# PIED PIPER CHILD

## Fragments from Another Life

## Ria Booth

# PIED PIPER CHILD

## Fragments from Another Life

### Ria Booth

EDITED BY AVALON WESTON

POBLESECBOOKS

Text: © Ria Booth 2018. The author's moral rights have been asserted.

Cover art, design, line editing and interior layout: © Poble Sec Books 2018.

Edited by Avalon Weston.

Published in ebook and print by Poble Sec Books in the United Kingdom in 2018. First edition.

All rights reserved. Without limiting the rights under copyright reserved above, no part of this publication may be reproduced, stored in or introduced into a retrieval system, or transmitted, in any form or by any means (electronic, mechanical, photocopying, recording or otherwise), without the prior written permission of the copyright owner and publisher of this book.

British Library Cataloguing in Publication Data

A CIP catalogue record for this book is available from the British Library.

www.poblesecbooks.com

ISBN: (print) 978-1-9999836-0-4;
(ebook) 978-1-9999836-1-1.

'Memory isn't fixed. It slips and slides about.'
 —Doris Lessing, *Time Bites*, 2004.

# EDITOR'S NOTE

This memoir was a pleasure to edit. All this editor did was eliminate repetition, create a sequence and add a few information boxes for the reader who may never have known or forgotten what, for example, a lock on the river is, or an off-licence was.

There are many records of the 1939 evacuation, but there can never be too many first-hand accounts of the individual experience. This is how history is made. Few, however, are prefaced by such a vivid picture of life before evacuation as is found in Ria's tricycle ride along the block of shops, which as a young child she knew so well.

Ria has a great deal more biographical material, so perhaps there will be a Volume Two, which will complete the story of her migrant experience and leave a full record for her descendants and all those historians interested in the phenomenon of voluntary migration.

It is interesting to speculate whether being transplanted at an early age facilitated in some way the decision in later life to move across the world and set up a home elsewhere.

I hope this memoir will take its place in the New Zealand archive of migrant experience.

—*Avalon Weston, editor*

# CONTENTS

| | |
|---|---:|
| PREFACE | 1 |
| RIA'S FAMILY TREE | 4 |
| CHATSWORTH ROAD E5 (A TRICYCLE TRIP) | 5 |
| 'EVACUATE FORTHWITH' | 17 |
| THE TRAIN JOURNEY | 19 |
| | |
| **THE FIELDS OF ENGLAND** | 23 |
| MEETING MRS BIRD | 24 |
| MRS BIRD'S COTTAGE | 27 |
| HIGH WYCH | 29 |
| WAR DECLARED | 33 |
| SCHOOL DAYS IN THE COUNTRY | 35 |
| MISS COLLIS | 37 |
| MR MABEY | 40 |
| MR BUTLER | 43 |
| MR BALL | 45 |
| WASHING | 48 |
| MARGARET | 50 |
| OUR CARAVAN | 52 |
| WINTER (1939-1940) | 57 |
| DAD UP FROM LONDON | 59 |
| 'THIS AWFUL COAT!' | 63 |
| OUT WALKING WITH DAD | 65 |

| | |
|---|---|
| JEAN MCGILL | 68 |
| BOOKS, NEWS AND OTHER ENTERTAINMENT | 70 |
| SOLDIERS AND REFUGEES | 73 |
| LAST GIRL IN | 75 |
| SNOW | 76 |
| TEA AT THE LODGE | 81 |
| THE CHRISTENING | 83 |
| HOME: AN ENDING AND A NEW BEGINNING | 87 |
| **HOME, YES AND THEN AWAY AGAIN** | 93 |
| FIRST YEAR AT OUR LADY'S CONVENT SCHOOL | 95 |
| SISTER LORETTA | 99 |
| SISTER URSULA | 103 |
| SISTER FREBONIA | 105 |
| OTHER TEACHERS AND AWARDS | 107 |
| FAMILY LIFE IN LONDON | 109 |
| OUTINGS | 112 |
| THE MYSTERY PLANE | 115 |
| **BACK TO HIGH WYCH** | 121 |
| THE ERRAND GIRL | 123 |
| FRESH CARAVAN, FRESH COMPANY | 126 |
| KITH AND KISSING COUSINS | 131 |
| FINAL FAREWELLS | 135 |
| WELWYN GARDEN CITY | 137 |
| CLACTON AND THE SHAKESPEARE AGAIN | 142 |
| APPENDIX: RIA'S FAVOURITE POEMS | 146 |
| REFERENCES AND ACKNOWLEDGEMENTS | 153 |

*Ria in 1938, aged seven*

# PREFACE

My stories about growing up in England may not be true at all, but they are how I remember them. Feelings about people, places and events still in my mind are my own authentic memories, pieces of a story about the past that I am writing for the future.

My parents, grandparents, their friends and relatives lived through events and told anecdotes that have stayed with me, and if I can manage to tell the story right, then their friends, fashions, London and country settings, in peace and wartime, will come alive for a while. They will cease to be serious old people, or young people in odd clothes, looking out from photographs at their descendants, but real people who had heaps of fun, heaps of trouble, and lived creative and imaginative lives.

The grandchildren and great-grandchildren who never knew them might one day be curious about them. I hope I can do their ancestors justice, as well as give some idea about growing up in England in the nineteen-thirties and forties.

What follows are my memories mainly of the war years, 1939 to 1945.

I am writing this in New Zealand, looking out across the hills of Hatfield's Beach, still topped by bush and close to a sheltered sandy East Coast bay. The bay is part of the Hauraki Gulf, the Hauraki Maritime Park which opens out to the South Pacific. As I remember the London streets and then the English village I came to know as a child, it feels almost like studying a Constable painting, *The Haywain*, say, with its memories of an England long past now. Layers of history are embedded in the streets and villages of my memory: thatched cottages, manor houses, garden pumps and traces of people who have lived before me.

I am curious about Ann Eastcott, a Cornish woman

*The Willis family, at the beach in July 1938: Ria's mother Bobby, her sister Jill, Ria (Pat) and her father Charles*

*The village of St Teath from the air, c. 1950s*

whose first son was John. And Sarah Fisher from Somerset, who went to London and married John's son, born in St Teath, Cornwall. He too went to London, but a few years before her. They were married at St Mary's Church, Spital Square, Whitechapel, London – formerly Middlesex. These are my great-grandparents, my maternal ancestors and my grandchildren's ancestors too.

I live in a land now where ancestors are a known and important part of who you are and where you are from. The Eastcotts, perhaps, were originally from the Dumnonii tribe of Cornwall, who came to be known as Celts – allied to the Celts of Brittany, Wales and Ireland – immigrants from Iberia perhaps, or the Atlantic coast of France.

*Pied Piper Child*

# THE WILLIS/EASTCOTT FAMILY TREE

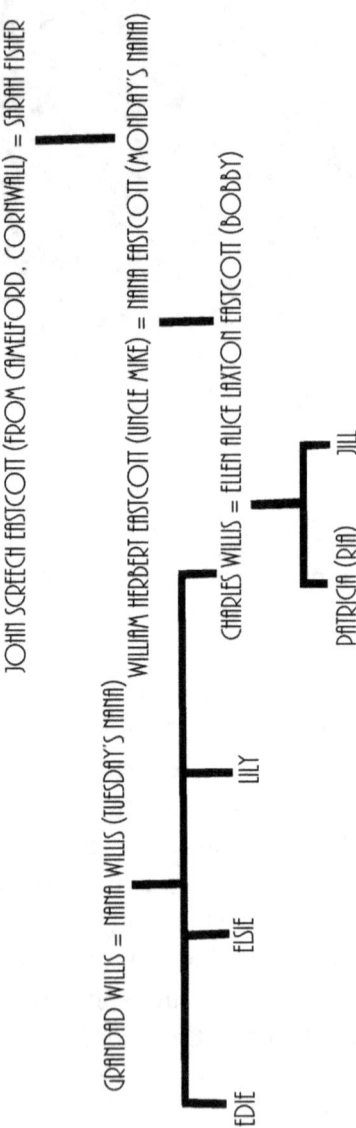

# CHATSWORTH ROAD E5
## (A Tricycle Trip)

> *Ria wrote this account of her street before her account of her evacuation. It is included here as it demonstrates so clearly the contrasts between town life before the war and village life, during evacuation.*

I do remember my first car – a blue tin model with pedals inside, which were supposed to move the thing if you peddled vigorously. It never got up to speed though, especially uphill, however hard I tried. But my most vivid memories of venturing out into the street, my bigger world, are of riding on one of those sturdy children's tricycles. I would ride it up and down 'our block' outside the shops. I'd freewheel to the downhill corner then turn round precariously, ready for the steady pedal back up.

The first, the corner shop on the steady climb, was a shop known as the off-licence, mysterious to me, often closed, but

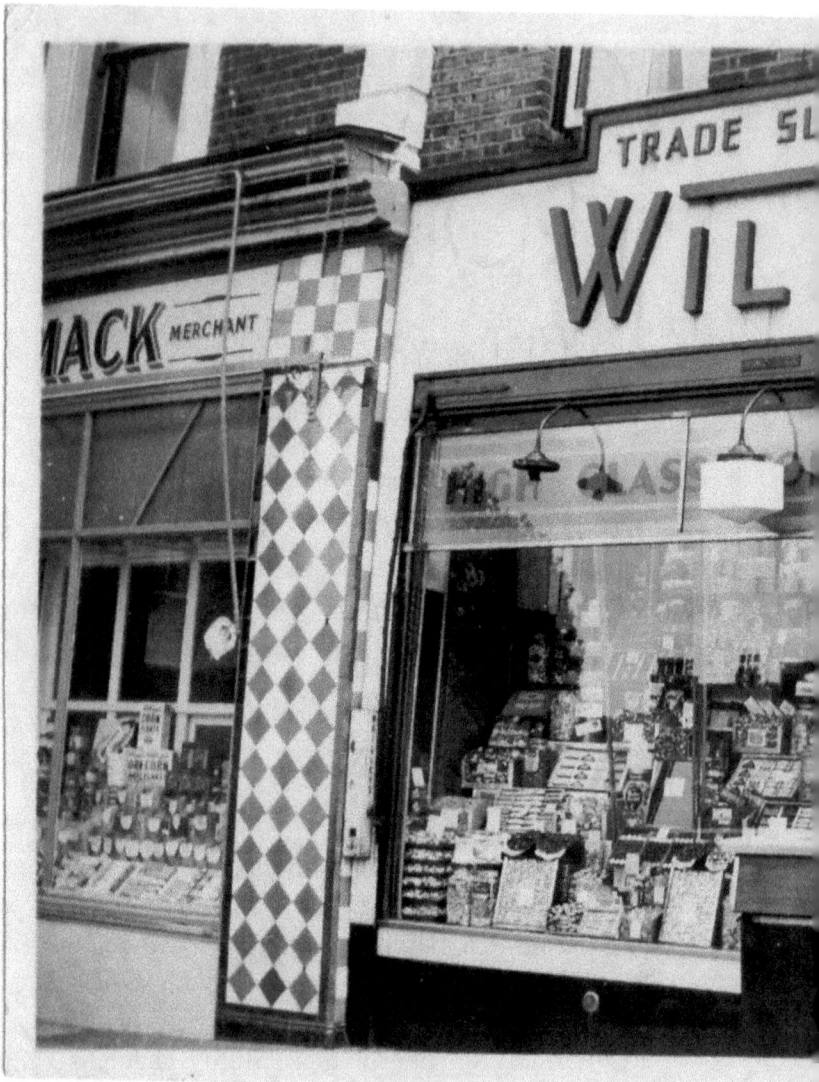

*The Willises' confectioner's, at 90 Chatsworth Rd, Hackney, E5, with Ria's parents, Bobby and Charles Willis at the ice cream stall. The phrase "Trade Supplied" on the façade indicates that Charles, who made his own*

*ice cream and other sweets, also acted as a wholesaler to other local shops. The three beautiful Art Deco lamps above the shop window are particularly striking* with counters so high that I couldn't see what they were selling when I did get to go in. My parents didn't drink much, just the occasional sherry, so they were not regular customers.

Our sweetshop, or 'confectioner's' as it was officially called, at 90 Chatsworth Rd, was about halfway up the road and one of a row of twelve shops which formed the front of a square block of terraced houses. Each shop had two floors above, a couple of rooms behind, and either a yard or small garden.

Shaw's corn chandler shop was next door to our shop, with yellow and white diagonal tiles around its windows and sacks of strange-smelling substances outside – birdseed, blood and bone, or lime for the garden, dog biscuits, and crackers for humans. We bought flour there and packaged goods, and food for our cats. When I think about it, I suppose my mother must have bought her groceries there, though I don't remember huge shopping

# THE OFF-LICENSE

*The concept was created by Gladstone's Licensing Act in 1860. The off-licence was a shop where alcohol could be bought for consumption off the premises – unlike a pub or restaurant which had to have a licence to serve alcohol on the premises. There would be shops on most high streets where alcohol could be bought outside pub-opening hours, for drinking at home.*

expeditions. As it was next door, she probably just popped in when she needed something. My grandfather, my father's father, had rented our shop before my dad bought it, but there was a romance, as Dad's sister, Elsie, married Len Shaw, son of the owner of the corn chandler. The ambience of that romance still seemed to hang in the air, so to speak, as we were always friendly with the owner of that shop when he visited. He must have been my Aunt Elsie's father-in-law.

A draper's shop was next to us on the other side, run by a young Jewish couple, Mark and Mrs Bogush. Mark and my father used to play tennis for a while. For some reason, we all called his wife Mrs Bogush. I don't think I ever knew her name. They eventually had a dear little girl called Valerie.

The oil shop was alongside them. I think nowadays it would be called a hardware shop or in England, still, an ironmonger's. The oil was paraffin, commonly used for heating then.

It used to run an outside stall too, selling wooden pegs, wooden and metal washing tubs and bowls. The lady of the store had a crippled arm, but still used to stand outside her shop, manning their stall, though she never looked very happy. There wasn't much to interest a four-year-old there, but next door to it there was the eel-pie shop.

Eels at the eel-pie shop! On market days, Thursday and Saturday mornings, most shops had a stall on the pavement in front of the shop. The eel-pie shop put out a trestle table on which were several dull metal trays. If I stood on tiptoes and peered into the metal trays, I could see eels – live, slithering, slimy eels with black shining skins and glittering eyes moving restlessly within the perimeter of the tray. If you decided to buy an eel – which we never did, thank God – the eel man, a kindly man called Arthur Toms, would lift an eel, cut off its head, chop it up still wriggling, and stuff it into a container of some sort. There was no plastic in those days, so perhaps it was oiled paper. I would watch in horror as he wiped his bloody hands on his white apron and knew I would never eat an eel as long as I lived.

If you were so inclined, you could go inside and sit at one of the enclosed, tall-backed, wooden benches and be served steaming-hot eel pie. People did and apparently went back for more, but I always thought they must have had tin stomachs. Our family was not an eel-pie family.

Arthur Toms, from the eel-pie shop liked to drop in for a chat and a cup of tea with my dad and mum at the end of the day and became a family friend. He was a gentle man, thin, with large ears, a pronounced nose and kindly eyes, who shared a story with a laugh in his voice, and enjoyed listening to an amusing tale. My mother was always happy to offer a cup of tea in our living room behind the shop. He used to call in after work before going home to Chingford to his wife, Lulu, who was small, buxom, with a strong voice and personality. They had a son, David, who became a psychiatrist. When I was older, I went to medical student

*An eel-pie shop – not the one on Chatsworth Rd, but perhaps similar to that which Ria knew*

balls with him a couple of times, and many years later, after his wife died, he went out with my sister Jill, too, for a time.

Next to the eel-pie shop – in the bloody centre of the block, so to speak – was the butcher, Mr Shaddick. He was a real butcher with a blue-and-white striped apron, standing behind the white marble counter-top; fresh, yellow sawdust covered the red floor. He was also rumoured to be a whiz with the share market and was liable to give his best customers market tips along with the sausages. He too put a couple of sons through medical school. His wife, who appeared rather severe, helped in the shop and I was in awe of both of them as they never seemed to smile much at the kid from the sweetshop.

They had five children, the youngest of whom was Tony, about my age. We played together and exchanged kisses in

*R. V. Shaddick's, the butcher's, now closed (2017)*

our backyard – his first as well as mine, I think. Perhaps that was why his mother was severe with me. I think the kiss was the result of being taken to see my first film, Rose Marie, a romantic musical starring Nelson Eddy and Jeanette MacDonald. I remember there was a lovesick Indian girl in it too, who didn't end up with Nelson Eddy.

Many years later, after the war, Donald, one of the Shaddicks' younger sons, brought back with him from Germany, where he had been part of the occupying army, a beautiful, gentle, golden-haired girl called Elsa. I used to feel so sorry for her having to work in the butcher's shop with her husband, who had taken over the shop by then. Eventually, she too must have felt the same, as she went back to Germany. It was a difficult time for a German girl to have started a new life in London.

The shopfront of the undertaker's, next to the butcher's, was black, opaque plate glass. Once or twice, I saw fabulous black-plumed horses drawing a gleaming black and glass hearse, but this later deteriorated to a sombre black car with silver sliders inside it, as Wilf Taylor, the undertaker, modernised his business.

Wilf was perfect for the part: tall, elegant in black tails and old enough to have silver hair. I later saw him in identical attire as Master, or more probably Grand Master, at a Masonic Lodge dinner. I often wondered at what stage he turned from a little boy or a teenager into this disturbingly sombre man, the image of death. Did he ease out of character at home or on holiday?

After the war, Wilf Taylor persuaded Arthur and my dad to join the masons. This led to some luxurious dinners and dances for my mother, and eventually me, every so often, when the masons threw a 'ladies' night' for wives, to compensate for the time their men spent away from home. My parents used to regard these things as part of my education, and certainly I enjoyed the food and the dancing. It didn't occur to me then that this was an all-male society. Any secret society is a mystery asking to be solved: what did they actually do? My father didn't stay a practising mason overly long. It probably intrigued him for a time, but I don't think he really cared much for such ritualised secret ceremonies.

A chemist (pharmacist) is a chemist anywhere, but this one between the undertaker and the toyshop also had a stall outside on market days, which sold sarsaparilla. It was good for you, the chemist thought, and I loved to drink a glass of

*Enid Blyton's Sunny Stories*

it. My mother was never really sure whether or not it was good for me, but I plagued her till a got a glass. It looked rather like Coca-Cola, but had a distinctive smell and satisfying taste. The chemist was a jovial man who wore a grey overall, but I never knew his name. Years later, my friend Joyce and I used to stop by for sarsaparilla from time to time, and he always perked up when Joyce came by – a pretty seventeen-year-old as she was then.

My beautiful toyshop was next. Here I lingered to look in the shop window, but you had to go inside to really appreciate the treasures there. I bought comics and Japanese flowers, marbles and paints, mosaics and kaleidoscopes, and books with pictures which were invisible till you scribbled in pencil over them. I loved going to see gentle-voiced, plump Ada, who had something wrong with one eye, which gave her an endearing look. I used to buy drawing books with my pocket money, and later *Enid Blyton's Sunny Stories*, a tiny weekly children's magazine, which was my great delight.

Lastly, on the top corner, was the dairy, white-tiled and perfect, staffed by milkmaids and lined with bottles of milk, cream and Tizer, a fizzy orange drink which was topped by one of those stoppers which look as if they were really meant to be an electric plug.

At that point, not being allowed to cross the road, I had to tricycle back down again, which was much easier than going up.

*Founded in 1924 and still on sale, "Tizer the Appetizer", is a citrus-flavoured soft drink bottled in Cumbernauld, Scotland*

*The Willises' shop, lit up at Christmastime, with festive decorations in the windows on each floor*

# 'EVACUATE FORTHWITH'

## 1 September 1939

On Thursday, 31 August 1939, at 11.07 am, Prime Minister Neville Chamberlain authorised the British Home Office to send a message to all schools within designated areas to carry out pre-arranged evacuation plans for children.

'Evacuate forthwith' was the terse message sent to 100,000 teachers in the many schools thought to be in danger of attack. Almost two million children were relocated.

We had had several practice runs before we actually went. My mother came up to the school with me each time, making sure I had my case, my gas mask and that everything was labelled. I remember waving a cheery goodbye to my dad, and setting off for the third time to the school. That was the actual day.

We left the shop, that morning and dad stood at the entrance watching us cross the road. I looked back and waved, I saw that Mark and Mrs Bogush from the drapers were there too, and Mrs Shaddick (the butcher's wife), and also Ada from the toyshop.

We walked on up to the school. I had my gas mask slung round my shoulder, and Mum was carrying my bag. We were joined by an elderly lady, a relative, I think, who I hadn't seen before; she came up and gave me a hug and kiss, and went back to stand next to my mother, who was trying to look philosophical but only succeeded in looking sad and serious.

We waited around in the playground till everyone had arrived and checked in. We were then shuffled into a crocodile and off we set, following the teachers. I waved to Mum and she waved too. Then the crocodile crawled, out of the playground, out of her sight, up the familiar road to Clapton Station. It was a long corridor of gas-mask-carrying, chattering children.

We walked to the station about ten minutes away, where a steam train was chuffing ready to go. The walk wasn't too far, just over a mile I suppose. I'd often done it with my father to catch the train to see 'Tuesday's Nana'. I used to be glad to hold his hand when the great engine chuffed into the station, whooshing clouds of white steam as it stopped.

My friend Jean McGill wasn't coming. Her parents wanted her to go to a Catholic school somewhere in the country. So Jean was not with me.

We didn't know where we were going. None of us, including our parents and teachers, knew where we were going. Not a clue. That was 1 September 1939. War against Germany was declared on 3 September 1939. I was eight years old.

# THE TRAIN JOURNEY

In those days, each carriage was divided into about five compartments and in each compartment were two, long, upholstered seats from side window to side window, so that you could sit facing the engine or travel with your back to it. We would rush to find an empty compartment with a window seat, and clang the heavy doors behind us before the whistle blew.

Today I was with a group of children, none of whom were the friends I had made that year.

We were all shepherded into the various compartments.

When I was four, mum had had typhoid and I had stayed with an aunt for several weeks. I thought I would soon be home again as my mother was quite well. This time, though I was a little scared, When I remembered the sad, serious look on my parents' faces, felt the gas mask in its green case swinging on my shoulder, and the apprehensive feeling in the air, I realised this was no ordinary school trip.

*London school children being evacuated, September 1939*

No one had known where we were going when we started out. Still no one seemed to know where we were going. Even now, in the train, we still did not know where we were going.

The train seemed in no hurry, chuffing slowly from the station, once we were all piled safely in it. Our teacher, Mr Butler was with a few of us in a small carriage. Some children were excited, others looked tearfully out of the window.

'There's our mothers, there, down there,' someone said, as we passed over a bridge.

'No, no, it isn't. Sit down.'

We all sat down. Mr Butler was tense and looking nervy. He too sat down and took off his shoes. A girl I didn't know then, said his feet were smelly and for some unknown reason, suddenly leaped forward and stamped on his foot. He shouted with pain; the group became subdued, apprehensive, but he just told her to behave and sit down. He thought it a good idea to unpack the lunches we had each brought with us. The train rumbled on without stopping at any stations.

Finally it did stop. We all tumbled out onto the platform. It was getting dark by then. A single

---

# Extract from the High Wych History Project Blog

*In the first week of September 1939, 175 evacuees (children teachers and helpers) from Millfields Junior School, Clapton, arrived on four double-decker buses from the Depot Station in Bishops Stortford. Accompanied by their head teacher Mr. R.H.Ball, they were greeted in High Wych by a delegation headed by Mrs Wentworth Stanley, the local billeting officer. ... Many of the children continued to be housed and educated within our Parish for the next four years or so.*

—Theo van de Bilt, High Wych History Project

decker bus was waiting for us and we were all hustled onto it. I think we were about thirty children, perhaps more. The bus drove through the dark and pulled up facing a short path which led into a hall. We thought we were still journeying on to somewhere else, perhaps just changing buses, but this was it. We had arrived. We clambered out of the bus into the cool night air and were guided into an open doorway.

Strangers were waiting for us in a hall. Our class stood in a straggly group along one side. On the other sat a row of women, eyeing us like goods at a market. As each name was called a lady got up, claimed a child or two, and shepherded them out of the hall. Where were they taking us?

Lastly, I suppose because my surname began with 'W', my name was called out. A tall, thin woman with stooped shoulders, grey hair in a bun, got up and walked towards me. Her eyes were smiling as if she knew I was hers. We must have had name tags on. Two more girls were called.

'Come along,' she said, 'I'm Mrs Bird.'

She led us out into the dark country night, all three of us trailing our cases and gas masks.

# THE FIELDS OF ENGLAND

## THE FIRST TIME AT HIGH WYCH

### 1 SEPTEMBER 1939

### UNTIL

### SUMMER 1942

# MEETING MRS BIRD

Mrs Bird led us into the night. A cheerful young woman with a strange accent was with us too. Mrs Bird introduced her as Cathie from next door. We crossed a road, unlatched a gate in a low picket fence, lifted the front door latch and trooped into a small room. Two men were there. Mrs Bird introduced us all.

'This is Rosie, and this is Pat, and this is … Pat.' *Two* 'Pats'! One was the girl who had stamped on our teacher's foot and the other was … me.

Mr Bird was silver-haired with a fine, thin silver moustache. He was stiff in his movements and rather grunty when he talked but he had smiley blue eyes. I learned later he had been a soldier. The other man was Sid, the lodger. He was young and tall with dark, unkempt hair, a bushy moustache and a lovely smile. He slept in the room next to this small living room and worked on a nearby farm.

'Is that Hitler?' A silly question. I knew he wasn't Hitler. He didn't look a bit like him. But everyone laughed.

Something furry brushed my legs. A dog.

'And this is Rex.'

He was a collie cross with thick curling, multi-coloured fur and silky ears. *Bliss!* I'd always wanted a dog.

Cathie made us a hot drink and settled us at the large table which almost filled the room. We sat then, that first night, in the table places that became our own while we lived in Mrs Bird's cottage.

A paraffin lamp with a pretty orange and cream shade stood in the middle as the only light. Later, Mrs Bird lit a candle and led us up worn, wooden, spiral stairs to a small bedroom in which was a double bed, then through into a tiny attic room, its sloping, beamed ceiling painted apple green. There was a double and a single bed.

'Who's the eldest?' asked Mrs Bird.

We all gave our birthdays. Rosie turned out to be the eldest by two months. She got the single bed. I shared with Pat.

*Mrs Bird outside her cottage, sometime in the late 1920s. The dog in her arms is not Rex but an earlier pooch*

# MRS BIRD'S COTTAGE

We were woken the next morning by the clucking of chickens. Apples on a tree outside our attic window were almost close enough to pick, exciting for young Londoners. Mrs Bird came in and filled the china basin on our dressing table with warm water for us to wash our faces and hands.

We ventured downstairs for breakfast. The kettle was boiling on a black coal range that stretched along one side of the living room. The large table, laid for breakfast, took up most of the rest of the room. In the front window, looking out onto the village green, hung a caged yellow canary.

'That's Joey,' Mrs Bird told us.

After breakfast – which was bread, buttered thinly by Mrs B before she sliced it, maybe plum jam, and maybe scrambled eggs, seeing the chickens lived there too – Mrs Bird took us, with Rex, outside in the sun. The cottage walls were washed white, and the wooden latched door was painted dark green. Purple clematis, flowering by the front door, spread over the thatched roof. An old iron pump seemed to grow in the corner of the front garden.

'You need to push hard down on this long handle to fill a jug or a cup with water,' Mrs Bird showed us.

A few soakings later, she decided to keep a jug of water for us in the house. The toilet was outside the back corner of the cottage, easier to find in the daylight than the previous night. Chickens were in a long wired run in the garden beside the cottage.

'That's clematis,' said Mrs Bird, pointing to the purple flowers climbing over the thatch, 'and this one here is called a Christmas rose, because it flowers in the winter. They're wallflowers there, and along the path are pinks in the spring. They smell beautiful. And those two big trees on the village green over the road are horse chestnuts. You'll get conkers there.'

'What are conkers?'

'You'll find out.'

The apples on the tree outside our window were sweet and crunchy. With the three of us asking questions, we soon learned Mrs Bird's history. She had been a maid in a big London house, where she had met Mr Bird. We thought she was old – sixty-five. She had had ten children.

'Ten! Ten! Where are they?'

'All grown up, Two are in the army. One of those is engaged to Cathie, the Scottish girl who was here last night. She looks after Lady Foot next door. The other is married to Margaret who has two little girls. She lives just outside the village up at the Manor of Groves. You'll meet her soon. Another son has a farm.'

'You've to go to school for a while,' Mrs Bird said, after she'd finished showing us outside. 'Then perhaps you can explore the village a bit.'

# HIGH WYCH

The school was just down the road, next to the church, and easy to find because several groups of children were heading in the same direction. It was built of the same local grey flint stone as the beautiful little church next to it. I remember each flint was smooth though uneven to touch, in shiny greys and blacks, but the raised edges could be sharp and they had a dry, flinty smell on a hot day. Like the church, the school had a red, tiled roof, and arched windows and doors.

We stood around in the playground for a time, talking in subdued voices, until Mr Ball and Mr Butler ushered us into the school itself. We shared desks because there weren't enough at that stage.

'This village is High Wych in the county of Hertfordshire,' they told us. 'School as usual tomorrow. Go back to your ladies today and write a letter home.'

Our foster mothers were always known as our 'ladies' from then on.

'What's your lady like?'

'OK. She's got ten children.'

'Gosh. Wish I had some other kids with me. My lady's

too fussy.'

A day off school! When they let us out, a group of us explored the village from end to end. It didn't take us long. I remember a boy called Alan Prestige was with us. He always made me laugh. This could be fun after all.

Beyond the school, houses petered out into woods and fields. We couldn't cope with woods and fields that day so turned the other way. There were large gates and a gravel road leading to a big dark house among the trees. We didn't like to venture into the grounds too far as it was obviously private. Past the school and church, we found The Rising Sun pub, set back from the road, almost opposite the church. Then past the little hall where we had arrived, we came back to the village green, with our cottage on one side, and another pub, The Half Moon, on the opposite side, with a small post-office-cum-shop a little further along.

Down a country lane and past houses, we found the entrance to a large park, flanked by tall iron gates, with iron bars flat across the entrance, which we later discovered were cattle grids. We explored a little way into this one. We could not see the house at all and there were cows there, eyeing us with interest, so we altered course smartly. Later we found these were the grounds of Lady Buxton of the Manor of Groves, and the first large house belonged to a Mrs Stanley.

'They're the "toffs",' said Mrs Bird, giving us our first lesson in the country class system.

A farm on the edge of the village looked interesting, but barking dogs, cows which could be bulls, and a threatening shout clearly meant we were not allowed in. Later on Alan managed to acquire a bike and amused us

*Mrs Bird's cottage and the green, c. 1911–1912, showing her and some of her sons, with The Half Moon pub sign centre left*

doing wheelies on the village green. He was a natural comedian, or I thought so. It was good to laugh.

Back in Mrs Bird's cottage, we wrote out letters home:

*Dear Mum and Dad,*
*We live in a cotij with a straw roof and a dog called Rex and a canary called Joey and a pump for water. Our lady is Missis Bird.*
*Luv Pat*

We took our letters to school next day and they were duly sent off, presumably with our addresses and where we were living. I'm sure our parents were relieved we were not far away – only about twenty-five miles from home. Some children were sent to Canada for the duration of the war.

## Rosie, another of Mrs Bird's evacuees, remembers

*I arrived in High Wych two or three days before war was declared and lived with Mr and Mrs Bird in their thatched cottage by the village green with two other evacuees. I was there for nearly three years. Living conditions were harsh. There was only one tap in the front garden and an outside toilet with no chain. Lighting was by oil lamps. We had (three of us evacuees) a weekly bath at another house in the village. The evacuees shared the village school with the local children at first, us in the mornings and them in the afternoons. Then change about the following week. This didn't work too well and soon wooden screens were put up to make more classes and we all went at the same time. We roamed the countryside around the village for many hours each free day and I greatly missed the countryside when I returned to London.*

—Rose Pocock, High Wych History Project

# WAR DECLARED
## 3 September 1939

War was declared on September the third, two days after we all left London. Place names were taken down or blacked out.

'Don't even tell anyone the way, or what the name of the village is,' they told us at school. 'They might be German spies.'

Rumours grew then about mysterious strangers who were definitely German, but could speak good English. The boys said how they had stalwartly and bravely refused to tell them that this was High Wych they were driving through.

'Sir, there were two spies in the village yesterday.'

'How do you know?'

'Well, Sir, they asked the way to Hoddesdon and wanted to know the name of the village.'

'You didn't tell them?'

'We said we didn't know, Sir.'

'Good.'

Slogans appeared and the whole country got to know them: 'Careless Talk Costs Lives'

*Pied Piper Child*

Mrs Bird had to put black-out material up at her cottage window as soon as it got dark. Not a crack of light must be seen by enemy planes. 'Dig for Victory' was another phrase, and many started growing vegetables in allotments when food rationing came in.

As the war progressed, 'Make do and mend' became the cry, as clothes rationing coupons were introduced. I learned to darn socks and knit pixie hoods at school – slowly and with great concentration.

Make Do and Mend, *a pamphlet issued by the British Ministry of Information in 1943*

# SCHOOL DAYS IN THE COUNTRY

Our teachers, who had come with us from London were Mr Butler and Mr Ball. The two resident High Wych teachers were Mr Mabey, the headmaster, and Miss Collis.

The schoolroom had been partitioned into three classes and we were in the middle one. Gothic windows only allowed soft light to filter through, so electric lights suspended on long cords helped us to read.

Mr Mabey with his country children had the classroom on our right side, and Miss Collis with her little five-year-olds had the class on our left. We London children were in the middle with our teacher, Mr Ball. The newly constructed partitions were of thin wood so it was easy to hear what went on in the other two classes. Miss Collis could be drilling her little ones through the two-times table, almost singing – 'three times two are six, four times two are eight' – soothing like a lullaby.

The older 'country' children, on the other side of our class, were taught by Mr Mabey. Mr Ball, one of our teachers, would close his eyes and our class would hold their breath as Mr Mabey exploded, sometimes throwing something at the back wall. I think he purposely never threw anything *at* anyone.

The first term of the English school year starts in September, so our practice walks around Millfields School playground back in Hackney must have taken place at the end of the long summer holidays. I think there were about thirty London children in our group. Both country and London kids had to learn to blend into one school. We settled together fairly well, I think, considering we townies had to cope with a new school, a new place and a new home, minus parents and other family members, while the country children had to accept us crowding into their school. Mostly we did as we were told in this novel situation.

Dig for Victory, *a campaign set up by the British Ministry of Agriculture in 1941*

# MISS COLLIS

Miss Collis was the teacher who gave me my most magical and memorable lessons. Although she was a buxom young woman, her dark eyes and sleek black hair drawn back into a bun gave her the look of a Spanish dancer, but she wore a practical, pale green overall for school, to protect her clothes from chalk dust.

She usually taught the five- and six-year-olds, but once a week she took the eight- and nine-year-old girls for sewing and knitting. The class was more inspirational than practical for us. I remember one late afternoon lesson was given to showing us how to 'turn' sheets when they started to wear in the middle.

'If a sheet wears in the middle,' she said, and she had a strong, musical voice with a Hertfordshire accent, 'you must turn it. You cut it down the centre and sew the good edges together in a flat seam.'

The sheet would be slightly smaller but would give a few months more wear. This was wartime, remember: 'Make do and mend' time. I think none of us in the class could even thread a needle at that stage, let alone manage a huge piece of material like a sheet. But we excitedly ran back to our respective 'ladies' to tell them how to do it.

Mrs Bird didn't have to comment on Miss Collis or her ideas as the humorous but mocking look in her eyes said it all. Neither she nor my mother took to the idea.

Winter was for knitting. The school supplied us with ropy wool in a dull, fawny colour and some thick knitting needles. We set out to knit 'pixie hoods'. These were a long length of stocking stitch, one plain, one purl, knitting which you then sewed up in the middle on one side at the back, to the length of your head, and the two ends became scarves. These took the whole of one winter, maybe two for some of us. You had to carefully note if you were to do a plain or a purl stitch, and if you didn't know, then you had to count the stitches from the beginning of the row to get it right, otherwise it showed up as a different pattern. Cathie, trying to keep a straight face, tried to explain to me, I remember, how you didn't need to count every time, as you could tell just by looking. But it never worked for me. It took two winters, and I think I wore it once or twice, but the wool was rough against my bare neck.

Then there was the frock. We must have been a little older even to think of such a thing. I believe Miss Collis cut them all out, and we sewed a few seams by hand. Short sleeves and pleats in front and back. Mine was a pale green, more eau-de-nil. I never ever wore it. I don't think my mother let me, because I was home before it was ever finished.

One spring day Miss Collis took us into the local woods for a nature lesson, London and country kids together. My father had taken me to Epping Forest near London, with its old oak trees and bracken-filled spaces. This small wood close to the school was quite different. Miss Collis called it a copse as it was just a small group of trees, though very old. She showed us where to find the clusters of dish-shaped leaves where purple violets hid. The scented air around gave them away. She managed to find clumps of pale yellow primroses too, pointing out the difference in the leaves, how the violets had deep green, dish-shaped leaves, and the primroses paler green, longer crinkly leaves. The country kids nodded knowingly as she showed us different trees and plants. There were hazels and alders, and along a stream, pale-green willows. Tall beech trees with smooth trunks, their dark green glossy leaves edged with fine hair, stood at the beginning of the wood, their tiny brown triangular nuts not yet ripe.

A few weeks later, we went to a bluebell wood, further away by Buxton's Farm. Between silver birches and alders, the floor of the wood was carpeted with misty blue flowers, an ethereal blue that seemed to float in the air, as far as you could see. Ancient as England. Magic to make you believe in fairies.

The scent of violets or a painting of a bluebell wood conjure in my mind now the picture of Miss Collis in her green overall, with her country sense and good nature. She started an interest in botany and nature for me which I've had all my life.

Mrs Bird said that Miss Collis had been engaged, or 'walking out' with a man for ten years. I was there three years and never saw him. I did hear later she had finally married and felt pleased for her.

# MR MABEY

Mr Mabey was the resident headmaster of High Wych Village School. He was energetic, in his early thirties, strong, stocky perhaps, with crinkly fair hair and blue eyes. He and his round-faced, dark-haired, softly spoken wife lived in the school house next door to the school.

He had a ten-acre voice which got louder when he became exasperated, which was often in those days. He caused the frail partition between the classes to shake. At that time, I was *so* glad I was not in his class, but the village children adored him. Our class knew when it was about to happen. We could feel the build-up. There was an impatient bark first of all, if he thought some boys at the back were not listening. The class would hesitate in whatever we were doing.

'Get on with your work,' Mr Ball would say firmly. 'Take no notice of what's happening anywhere else.' But he would straighten the papers on his desk and sometimes get off his stool waiting for the explosion. Both classes would grow quiet. Then *crash!* – the sound of a book being thrown or a piece of chalk hitting the back wall – and Mr Mabey's ten-acre voice would bellow after it. It was like a small earth tremor at one end of the hall. No one ever seemed to know exactly what caused it. Then it would subside and we would all settle down after this exciting little grown-up drama. I was so glad I was not in his class. I would have settled for the *Ten Commandments* any day rather than being shouted at and having things thrown at me.

Then came the shock announcement. Heads had conferred and decisions reached. We were told we were to have some lessons with Mr Mabey the following week. They were amalgamating two classes, since some children and Mr Butler had gone back to London. They thought it better for us to mix with each other. I was apprehensive and didn't look forward to the next week at school.

That weekend, I was walking back to Mrs Bird's on my own and had to walk across the fields by myself. There were often cows in the Stile Meadow, but generally on the far side, well away from my path, and I often took the long way round the field to avoid them. We had been told that if planes flew low over the village, we were to just lie flat on the ground and not move. I used to pray no planes would choose that moment as there was no way I was ever going to lie flat among those cows.

This time, to my horror, there were twenty or so cows in the field *between* me and the stile to the road, looking up and gazing soulfully at me, stopping their chewing to regard me.

I dithered around, thinking how huge they were and that they could run faster than me, knowing they were often curious and playful and followed you *en masse*. I thought I'd wait till they moved away from the stile in search of fresh grass, but they didn't. They just stood staring at me.

Suddenly someone shouted:

'Come on. Wave your arms. Yell at them. Just walk across.'

It was Mr Mabey. He stood there on the other side of the field by the road, waiting for me to cross. He and I knew if he walked towards me, the cows would walk in front of him towards me too. I gathered my courage and walked. As I got nearer I waved my arms. The nearest cow shied away, bumping the next animal as it did so, which also turned away. Amazed, I shouted louder and waved my arms again. The herd scattered, lolloping clumsily, right and left. So this was the nature of cows. I shouted and waved my arms again as they turned tail and scattered. I ran towards the gate. Mr Mabey was laughing, but not at me.

'That's the way. Show 'em who's boss. Same with horses.' He grinned as I stood there smiling and only a little shy now. He did have a friendly face after all. 'You're all right now, aren't you? See you Monday.'

He got back into his car.

'Yes Sir. Thank you, Sir.'

I turned on my way to the village. I wasn't frightened of cows now and I wasn't frightened of Mr Mabey either. School the next week was not going to be so bad after all, maybe even fun. I was forever grateful. Mr Mabey became my favourite teacher in those few minutes. I thought he was pretty neat and was sorry when he was called up to join the army. What a senseless war. I notice on the map there is now a Mabey Walk in High Wych, which I don't remember being there before. I do hope he got back from the war safely.

I realised as I write this how difficult it must have been for both schools to share the same small building under such makeshift conditions.

# MR BUTLER

Our own teacher, Mr Butler, was about fifty, with grey, thinning hair, thick glasses, and an odd way of walking with stiff neck and chin jutting forward. He always wore grey – grey jacket, grey trousers – and his lessons were grey too. He came from Yorkshire, I believe, and had a mild accent, though slightly nasal.

Mr Butler went back to London after a few weeks or months, I'm not sure how many. Perhaps there simply was not room in the school for both him and Mr Ball. And Mr Ball had his family with him. I didn't see Mr Butler again for some time, but years later, it was he who recommended the convent school my parents sent me to, and then turned up to try and give me some Latin lessons a few times.

In the first few weeks or perhaps months that we were settling into High Wych, Mr Butler used to take the three of us girls from Mrs Bird for country walks to explore the area. We didn't really need or want him, but I think he felt this sort of duty to my father to 'keep an eye on me'. We certainly explored the area, going on long walks together, but we three girls led him a merry dance, particularly Pat and I. Rosie was a rather melancholy girl, always homesick and never really happy, but longing for her mother to come and get her. Her mother had been a model. Rosie was tall and thin too, and would probably be a model too, she told us.

Pat on the other hand was a tough little character. She too wanted to go back home, but to her 'Gran'. She never mentioned her parents at all. She made the best of things and we rubbed along quite well most of the time, though we were very different. She got surly and grumpy when she was unhappy, which was often.

We had acquired gum boots by then, or wellies – Wellington Boots as they are called in England. Having

*The British Saddleback would be the pig Ria refers to*

discovered there were bountiful gurgling streams in the country, and trees to climb, we led Mr Butler along them, with his trousers coiled round his white legs and his shoes and socks soaking, despite his careful footwork. I think we knew exactly what we were doing. We had wonderful walks, discovering pigs for the first time – those half pink and half black pigs they rear there, and getting to know the names of the various farms and woods around the village.

# MR BALL

Mr Ball had been the headmaster of our Millfields Junior School in Clapton. He had two teenage daughters, the talk of the village because they wore eye shadow in a dark, purply colour which made them look as if they hadn't slept for weeks. There was, after all, nothing in the *Ten Commandments* about eye shadow or the wearing of it. One of them scandalised the village later when she was reputed to have dated an American soldier. We never saw Mrs Ball, who must have kept a low profile.

I was rather in awe of Mr Ball, remembering the twice-weekly assemblies of the whole school there when he used to get us to recite the *Ten Commandments* with little bits of sung verse in between. He was round and short, so of course we called him 'Ballee'. Cultured and softly spoken, he took us for English and Music.

Sometimes at playtime, school playtimes, Mr Ball played the old upright piano in the middle classroom. He used to try out various songs he was going to teach us from the song-books he had, choosing those he considered suitable. He left out the love songs, the drinking songs and stuck to sea shanties and going-to-market songs. I liked to sneak to the doorway and watch him playing. We were not allowed to touch the piano though.

In the afternoon, we would have a singing session and learn all the old English, Irish, Scottish and Welsh folk songs: *Cockles and Mussels, The Minstrel Boy, Loch Lomond, Danny Boy, Riding Down to Bangor, The Duke of York's 10,000 Men, Skye Boat Song, Greensleeves, My Bonny Lies Over the Ocean, Bobby Shaftoe, Scarborough Fair, Shenandoah* and something about the washing on Monday, ironing on Tuesday ... All three classes joined in.

I would love to trace some of the poems we read together, such as 'Berries' by Walter De La Mare:

*There was an old woman*
*Went blackberry picking*
*Along the hedges*
*From Weep to Wicking*

and

*... Plunder of April's gold we sought,*
*Little of April's anger thought,*
*Caught in a copse without defence,*
*Low we crouched in the rain-squall dense ...*

from 'The Adventurers' by Sir Henry Newbolt, or 'Old Nicholas Nye' ... who it turned out was a donkey.

All were humorous or whimsical poems with simple language, great rhythms and rhymes. We used to read them out loud together, while he would beat time with his hand on his tall wooden desk. On the other hand, he could be quite dismissive. I remember wanting to learn a poem called 'London Snow' – rather long for my age group, but I knew the first few lines. Standing up in class, I forgot even those for a moment. I was about to go on as they came back into mind when he just said, 'I think that was too long for you.' And I had to sit down.

*The Appendix on page 146 contains a selection of Ria's favourite poems.*

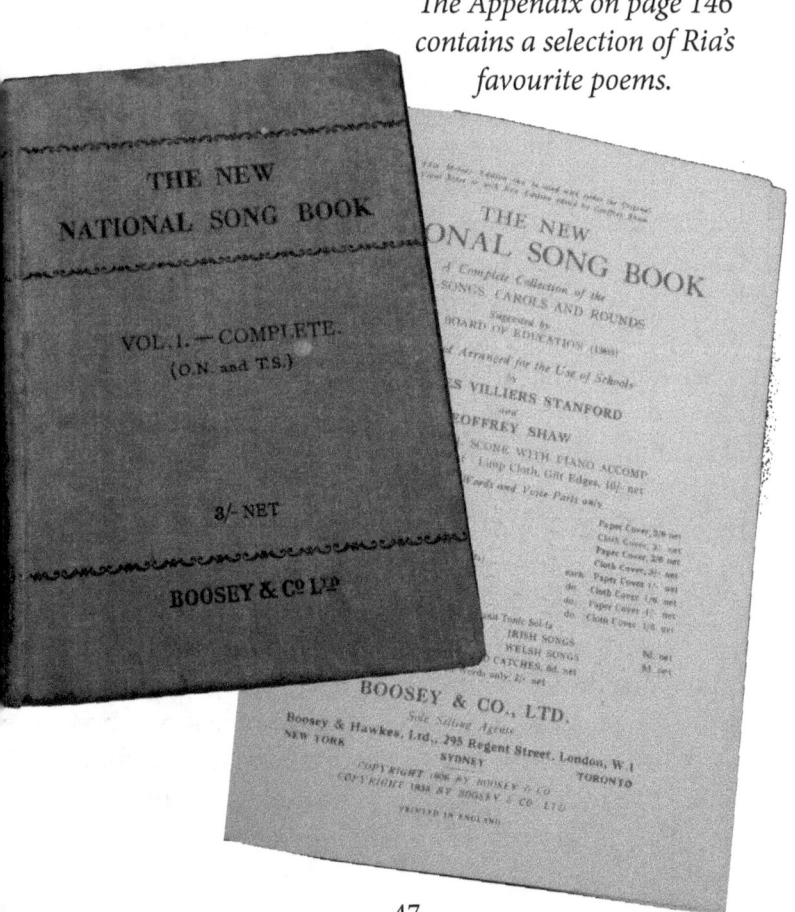

# WASHING

On my first summer at High Wych, I somehow had acquired a cotton frock in a red pattern with a white panel down the front. (Whoever gave that to a nine-year old must have been out of their mind!) Mr Ball called me over one lunchtime and suggested I make sure it was washed. What a dilemma! Did he really expect me to confront Mrs Bird and tell her my frock was dirty? She did all our washing by hand – no washing machines then, no hot water except what could be boiled on the range. What a stupid man! I think I was going on nine then, quite old enough to wash something given facilities to do so, but not in someone else's house. I think I did mumble to Mrs Bird what he had said, and she was rightfully scornful, but I know she understood and didn't blame me.

I suspect we were all pretty grubby most of the time. Mrs Bird brought up a basin of water to our bedroom each day to wash our faces and hands. Once a week we were sent to a house up the road a bit for a bath – five inches of water to be shared by the three of us. (The Ministry of something had commanded everyone use only five inches in their baths.) The house was a very clean, modern, suburban-type house with a built-in bath in its own bathroom. Quite different from Mrs Bird's homely little cottage where the only water source was the outside pump in the front garden. The extremely clean lady who supervised our bathing and hair-washing was quite shocked, I remember, to discover none of the three of us had separate cloths for tops and bottoms. Very clean, she was, but not endowed with empathy or imagination.

As I said, there were about thirty children in our group, but later, some children were taken back to London to be home. Others were expected to stay, but did not like it. The Levi brothers, Nevil and Maurice, were always planning a getaway and ran away several times, making exciting news for those of us who stayed. They were finally successful.

We three little girls, Rosie, Pat and I, were fortunate with 'our lady', Mrs Bird. We walked the few minutes back to the cottage for lunch, our main meal each day, and I don't remember ever being hungry. Mr Bird grew vegetables in his allotment and we had bubble and squeak, carrots, and my favourite, mashed swedes, orange and sweet. Sid sometimes went out and shot us a rabbit for our tea.

# MARGARET

After school we walked through the park to the Manor of Groves, where Mrs Bird's daughter-in-law Margaret lived. She was young and energetic and had two small children – Jasmine, three and Margaret (Maggie), eighteen months.

Margaret lived in the keeper's lodge at the Buxton Manor estate known as the Manor of Groves. Her husband, Henry, one of Mrs Bird's twin sons, was a soldier at the war. I don't know where he was stationed. We never saw him. Neither did poor Margaret.

The three of us used to walk through the village after school, through the great iron gates of the estate, across the cattle grid, all new to us townies, into meadows with huge old shade trees growing here and there, acting as shade for the cattle.

We followed the narrow gravel road till we crossed the second cattle grid and found ourselves in a tall, dark beech wood. Ten or fifteen minutes walking through there, and we were at Margaret's place, in the corner of a gravel yard edged with stables for horses and carriages, and small dusty copses of yew and fir trees.

Margaret was a naturally cheerful lady and the babies liked to see us. I think we mostly had jam sandwiches or crackers and played outside making pretend houses for ourselves in the copses with the spicy-smelling dust for boundaries, reading or playing with Jasmine and Maggie till it was time for their bed. Then we went home to Mrs Bird's cottage, sometimes braving the beech woods in the dark.

*The Manor of Groves is now a hotel, catering to weddings, conferences, events and team-building days*

# OUR CARAVAN

Once Mum and Dad knew where I was, they drove down to find me. I think they shut the shop as usual on a Thursday, or sometimes perhaps on a Sunday, as sugar became scarce and their trading hours shorter. (Sugar rationing was introduced on 8 January 1940. The allowance was 8 oz per person per week.)

When they drove up to see me at High Wych, they must have found a babysitter for Jill as I don't remember seeing her. We would drive, go for a walk and explore the area a bit before they had to go back home and leave me with Mrs Bird. Perhaps they didn't come so often because of the shop, or because I could have been upset not to go home again.

Dad was anxious to get Mum and Jill out of London. An English ship, the *Athenia*, had been sunk off the coast of Ireland by a German U-boat, and although the London Blitz did not start until September 1940, there was much talk of imminent bombing.

> # THE SINKING OF THE ATHENIA
> ## 3 SEPTEMBER 1939
> *The Athenia was torpedoed, in error, it is thought – the German U-boat thinking it was a military ship when in fact it was a passenger vessel. The 93 who were lost were perhaps the first casualties of World War Two. Because the ship sank very slowly, over 1000 people were saved. Canadians and Americans were among those who died. There were newspaper headlines such as 'Empire at War'. It was a memorable incident in the zeitgeist of the time.*

Finding digs for a mother and a two-year-old was difficult, but Dad had an idea – a caravan. If a caravan could be bought and somewhere found to locate it near me, then the family could stay in touch. He and Mum searched every week until finally they found a farmer willing to let us put a caravan on his land, about two miles by road from High Wych.

Mr Hipwell, of Redericks Farm near Harlow, showed us a tiny enclosure between a muddy lane and a field, used as a cattle enclosure. It was bordered on one side by a hazel copse and the other by a ditch, then a small grassy enclosure with some apple trees,

*The caravan that Ria's parents parked at Redericks Farm, with Charles and Bobby crouching under the trees beside it*

which led by means of a stile into a plum orchard and then to the farmyard itself. Perfect! In no time Dad had located a tiny, egg-shaped wooden caravan and had it put on foundations. It was fenced off from the field by a barbed wire fence, and from the lane by a five-barred gate. Cows were brought in from the river meadows, up the lane to be milked at the farm; we quickly learned to step carefully.

Mum and Jill moved into the caravan. It could sleep the four of us at weekends, with one double

*Redericks Farm, in Harlow, as it looked in 1940*

*Left: The caravan, showing (left to right) Ria's Nana Eastcott, her mother Bobby, her sister Jill and herself, c. 1944*

bed and two bunks, and we could fill up two large bottles of water from a tap in the farmyard and so cook meals and brew tea. During the week, when Dad was in London and I was at school in High Wych, Mum and Jill were there by themselves.

In the evenings, they wended their way, at Jill's two-year-old pace, up the lane into a country road, where down a bit further were a few houses. A friendly family there had agreed to let Mum and Jill have a bedroom to sleep in at night. The lady of the house had a little boy called Aubrey.

*Jill and Ria in the field beside the caravan, summer 1940*

# WINTER
## 1939-1940

That 1939–1940 winter was one of the coldest and longest for forty-five years, with seemingly endless snowfalls creating snowdrifts higher than children, higher than adults. Boots, scarves and gloves became part of our lives.

Italy too became the enemy as it signed a pact with Hitler. Nobody knew what was going to happen. Holland was invaded, then parts of France. Dunkirk was being planned. England was thinking it would be next.

German bombing raids over English seaports and over London began. The English Royal Air Force was pitifully small. Young men, some as young as eighteen, were called up to train as pilots and fly the Spitfires and Hurricanes to make some sort of fight against them. In the ensuing Battle of Britain, as it became known, they did fantastically. They became a legend.

'Put that light out!' became the call. Not a crack must show. Even Mrs Bird in the country had to black out her windows at night so no glimpse of the paraffin lamp beams from her table could shine out. The whole of the village of High Wych and outlying farms lay in darkness.

*Bobby and Jill outside the caravan, and waving goodbye to Charles, winter 1940*

# DAD UP FROM LONDON

Dad often cycled the twenty-five miles from London if he did not have petrol as it was rationed. Mum was always relieved when he appeared. She had no telephone and therefore never knew if he had survived the night raids. So if he suddenly arrived at the five-barred gate, she could just as well burst into tears as show her pleasure in a hug and kiss.

With the arrival of the caravan, my weekends back at High Wych took a turn for the better. Dad was shown a short cut over the fields from the farm to the village, so he could walk over to collect me on the Saturday, then return me on the Sunday night ready for school next day. After a while, I got to know the way myself and could make my own way across the fields. He always brought me back though and made sure I was safely installed in the cottage again.

I grew to love that walk over the fields. I can do it in my imagination even now and know all the hedgerow plants and flowers along the way. I'd set out from the cottage, clicking the gate behind me, walk down through the village, past The Rising Sun, past the church, the school, right to the end of the village, where Miss Collis's copse started. Just down on the left was the Stile Meadow, or the Star Meadow as I thought it was then. You climbed the five-bar gate, walked right across the

*Jill and Charles before the caravan, winter 1940*

field, hoping there were no too-friendly cows there, climbed over the wooden stile, worn silver, through to the Corn Meadow. In the left corner was an elderberry bush, covered with white flowers in spring. If the corn was newly planted and green, or growing golden and tall, you had to walk the two sides of the square field. I knew every bush and tree in the hedgerows. I knew the elder bush by the stile, the hawthorn, the taller oak trees, the old man's beard bushes in the hedge, and the beautiful, haunting dog-roses, so simple yet so perfect. I knew the birds that lived there. I could spot a rabbit or a pheasant.

In late summer, once the grain, usually wheat, was cut and stacked into stooks, I could cross the field diagonally, and loved to tread down on the prickly stubble. If it had been raining, it would squirt water back up your boots or bare legs.

The next field grew sugar beet for the cattle. A scarecrow was there for a while, reminding me of Worzel Gummidge; Rather, years later, reading *Worzel Gummidge* reminded me of that scarecrow.

Then came a few farm workers' cottages on the right, and a smaller field, sometimes planted with barley or oats – and by then I knew the difference. Next, you turned left onto the country road for about twenty paces, then right into the cattle lane running down to the river from Redericks' farmhouse.

The farm was a beautiful, small mixed farm, growing various crops as well as several fruit orchards and about twenty or thirty milking cows – twenty probably, as they all had names: Daisy, Bluebell, Buttercup, Big Eyes, Brownie. There was also a small flock of sheep and two beautiful Clydesdales, working horses who pulled the carts filled with hay or wheat.

They had a dog too, always chained up near the farm house, which barked loudly at me when I went to collect water in the two glass bottles – one of my jobs. The dog might have been friendly if he hadn't always been on guard.

Dad put up a canvas shelter in front of the caravan to keep the ground dry in winter, but my poor mother must have been at her wits' end to keep two-year-old Jill amused and healthy. They would go for walks around the field in front of the caravan, collecting whatever was in season, of which more below.

# Worzel Gummidge

*Worzel Gummidge, by Barbara Euphan Todd was published in 1936. In 1941, it was the first paperback published by Puffin. So the book was around when Ria saw the scarecrow in the 1940s, but it never came her way. The stories continued to appear for many years, adapted for radio before the war and on TV in the 1950s and 1980s. The children's TV series was at one point made in New Zealand (1987–1989).*

# 'THAT AWFUL COAT!'

Mum knitted and sewed, as she always had done, and sewed us clothes when she could procure material. She acquired some light-blue woollen material with a large tartan-like red-and-blue plaid on it, and made me a winter's coat with a hood. I just loved it. The hood was lined, the coat warm, and certainly unique, but material of any kind was scarce. Our mother possibly came by this from Soapy Joe, our local black market dealer. You got what you could. With no electricity and therefore no sewing machine in the caravan, Mum must have made that coat, stitching it by hand, which she was well able to do. The lady in the house where she and Jill slept might have had a sewing machine, but I think Mum would have sewn it herself – something to do in the lonely day.

My sister rang me recently:

'We've found this old photo of you in that awful coat!'

Indignantly, I explained: 'Mum made that coat for me in the big snow winter – you were only two. It was pale blue with a large tartan check. It was wool. You couldn't get materials then, so you couldn't be choosy. And she made me that coat. It was warm, and I loved it.

So in the winter of the big snow, I had a warm coat, boots and gloves. What more could I ask for? But as time went on it seemed to get shorter and shorter and was soon above my knees.

*Ria wearing 'that Awful Coat!', with her younger sister Jill. Aubrey, the boy from the house where Jill and Bobby slept at night, is in the caravan doorway*

# OUT WALKING WITH DAD

Dad enjoyed his short spells of country life too, peaceful after the London nights of bombing, so when he arrived at weekends he made the most of the change.

In autumn, blackberries can be gathered if you could find a hooked stick to pull down the top branches with the juiciest berries on them. There were also two mature walnut trees at the top of the field, so you could pick up the nuts in their green cases when they fell from the tree, and split them to reveal the striated brown walnut shell enclosing its wrinkled, milky nut.

Dad asked Mr Hipwell about the walnuts dropping from the trees and Mr Hipwell told him to help himself. Fresh walnuts are *manna* from heaven, nothing like the dried-up kernels you buy in today's supermarkets. Dad found a good recipe and pickled quite a few jars: delicious in a salad or sandwich, or with cheese when we could get it.

And in autumn too, 'seasons of mists and mellow fruitfulness', we found early-morning fresh mushrooms, white and creamy, growing in circles round the cow pats. Dad occasionally procured some black-market bacon, probably from Soapy Joe in exchange for sugar or chocolate, and we'd feast on fried farm eggs, bacon, and freshly picked and sometimes peeled – they grew through cow pats, remember – mushrooms.

There were also hazel nuts ripening in the thicket by the caravan, and the blackberries to be picked, and plums and apples falling off the trees in the orchard. One bumper year, Mr Hipwell invited the children of High Wych School to come and pick their fill to take home.

Our great delight in summer weekends, was to walk down to the River Stort. Our caravan was on a hill above the river. We could walk across the sloping field diagonally, thread through a gap in the hedge to the marshy fields bordering the river, where Mr Hipwell's sheep or cattle grazed, then walk the short distance along the tow-path to the footbridge where you could cross the river to the far bank. Behind a corrugated-iron fence painted green, a small inlet had been turned into a swimming pool complete with

*Harlow Mill Lock House in 1903*

# LOCKS

*Locks are a method of allowing river or canal boat transport of goods regardless of topological difficulties. Boats are raised or lowered using a series of gates and pools. They exist extensively along the Thames and its tributaries.*

changing sheds and a shallow children's area. There, in the green, muddy-smelling river water, I learned to swim. *Bliss!* On a hot summer's day, Dad and I walked down to swim. Mum was never so keen, but came with us down to the riverside once Jill was old enough to walk the distance.

Dad and I used to walk to the next lock sometimes, Burnt Mill lock I think it was, the one after the Harlow Mill lock.

He pointed out blue-winged dragonflies hovering above the water, and occasionally the flash of a turquoise kingfisher. It might have been his first time seeing these wonders, as well as mine.

I understand the nature walk along the River Stort towpath is still beautiful and the river is used now by holiday barges and boats.

One evening, we spotted a sheep fallen into the river, its feet stuck in the mud though it was struggling to get out. Dad sent me up to the farm to get the farmer while he got into the water to try to get the soggy sheep out. Luckily, Peter, the farmer's son, was home and came down to the rescue with a rope and the animal was pulled out with great effort.

# JEAN MCGILL

School at the village that summer wasn't so bad either. One delightful morning, Jean McGill appeared at school. Her first place of evacuation had not been at all happy, so her mother brought her to High Wych. Sadly, this next lodging was not much better. Her landlady, Mrs D, was very strict, especially about Sundays.

'Mrs Bird, can I go up to Mrs D to play with Jean after school?'

Mrs Bird looked doubtful.

'… But please, she's my best friend at home. We always play together.'

Mrs Bird agreed a little grudgingly. She knew Mrs D better than me.

I went. We were not allowed in the house, or out of the garden. As far as I remember, there was nothing to eat. We stayed in the garden. Mrs D stayed in the house. I don't remember playing there much since there was such a loaded atmosphere.

A week or so later, Dad and Mum invited Jean to come over with me so we could all go swimming together. Jean wanted to come, but Mrs D would not allow her to as it was Sunday. Poor Jean. She must have been able to come sometime, as to this day she remembers our 'caravan in the woods'.

We couldn't play after school as I was at Margaret's, but we had fun at school. We played something on (pretend) horseback involving breadfruit as I remember. (I still haven't seen or tried a breadfruit, which is grown throughout Oceania, though not in New Zealand, but it sounded exotic then.) It's not surprising we didn't hit on bananas as they were just as unavailable then.

We founded 'The Green Feather Club', says Jean. A classmate joined the club too: Irene Elvin. Shorter than most of us, she was nick-named 'Titch'.

(She made up for that later when she grew up into a stunning seventeen-year old with blonde hair, large eyes and a rich singing voice. We got together as I played piano and she sought an accompanist. I hate accompanying – those wanting accompaniment assume you can play anything from jazz to opera to classics of all sorts and sizes at the touch of a piano key. Irene came to a party I had, chatted up a boy I liked, and sat on his knee the whole evening flirting. End of friendship.)

*Jean McGill and her mother, 1938*

# BOOKS, NEWS AND OTHER ENTERTAINMENT

One day, at school, a small truck drove into the playground and the teachers unloaded two large wooden crates, depositing them on the school floor in front of the class. We gathered round as they were opened.

Books! Dozens of them. Picture books, reading books, puzzles and poetry books.

'This is your library. You are allowed to take home one book a fortnight. If you bring it back in good condition, you may then choose another.'

What bliss! Library day. We anticipated it with huge pleasure. Some of us were allowed to choose two. We had no TV, no nearby cinema, no videos, no portable music or radio, except the household radio belonging to our landlady. Some of us had plasticine, or games or crayons sent from home. Once the blackout curtains were up in the evenings, not a crack of light showing from outside, there was nothing to do but what we could imagine. And so we had our books until bed.

The war made itself known sometimes.

Italy became the enemy as it signed a pact with Hitler. Nobody knew what was going to happen. Holland was invaded, then parts of France. Dunkirk was being planned. England was thinking it would be next.

Occasionally there were 'dog-fights' far up in the sky, as young men in their teens and twenties, piloting Spitfires, tiny dots glinting silver in the blue sky, drove back enemy planes trying to bomb our towns and airfields. Hoddesdon Airfield was fairly close. We never saw any actually shot down, though plenty were. An early warning system had been set up in various places near the coast so that as soon as a German plane crossed into our airspace, the young RAF pilots would race to their parked planes to do battle. This time we won, and the Nazis did not take over Britain.

Another time we saw squadron after squadron of fighter planes and bombers steadily droning their way south-west. I think we'd never seen so many planes.

'Something big happening,' said Dad speculatively, as we all gazed upwards. We heard the news the next day.

Then, of course, we had to be quiet for the News, particularly the nine o'clock.

News was all-important. The names of the war flashed past us without any meaning. Dunkirk, Vichy Government, Berlin, Vladivostok, Poland, though we all knew Hitler and Goering and Goebbels – the real baddies. I remember the names of BBC newsreaders, Stuart Hibberd and Alva Liddell:

'This is the BBC Home Service with the nine o'clock news. This is Stuart Hibberd reading it.'

During the day, my mother was alone with Jill in the caravan. She needed entertainment of some kind. She had a little portable radio, but that was more background company. She and Jill could take short walks round the field, picking flowers, blackberries, whatever was in season. There was no room for a piano, but Dad bought her a guitar. Unfortunately, he chose a steel-strung guitar. The strings, I should imagine, were too hard for Mum's fingers and the guitar is a hard instrument to teach yourself, with no one to compare notes with. In the end, Dad took it home to Chatsworth and started to play with it himself, finding he liked it very well.

From there, possibly buying strings in a music shop, he came to the idea of a ukulele, then popularised by George Formby. He bought one and an instruction book to go with it.

Whether he offered it to Mum, I don't know, but he gave it to me one weekend. I was enchanted with it. I had a little four-tube blow-pipe tuner to go with it, though I doubt if I ever got it completely in tune. *Swanee River* was the first song in the book, followed by *Drink To Me Only with Thine Eyes*, two horribly dreary songs, but I plucked away and learned the chords and how they worked and spent happy hours in my bedroom at Mrs Bird's (the others had gone home by then), or in a country lane, strumming away and singing.

*A 1942 mobile library, this one at Nonington, donated by the YMCA for the British Armed Forces*

# SOLDIERS AND REFUGEES

One morning in our first year at High Wych, we could not cross the road to the village green because of the convoy going through. Army trucks rumbled slowly past, one after the other, filled with young men in uniform. We thought there were hundreds of them, trucks, that is, and we waved to all the young men in them. Some of them waved back, others didn't. They just sat there. They didn't know where they were going, just as we hadn't known where we were going a few months earlier.

While we waited, the 'refugees' came by us, walking slowly. Pat stared, open-mouthed. Sometimes she did that in a truculent sort of way, and unkind, I thought. These people coming towards us were not happy.

One was a stocky man, middle-aged with a red face and thick glasses. I thought he was quite ugly. He walked with a stick, very carefully. He'd had a stroke, they said. His wife supported him with her arm under his. She was silver-haired and always beautifully groomed, but as she was taller than he, she had to stoop to support him. She was fair-skinned and blue-eyed. She gave me a lovely smile but quickly turned her eyes from my staring classmates.

They were German, our 'lady' said: Mr and Mrs Goldschmidt. They had had to leave all their money in Germany and come here to England. We knew all this because they were billeted next door to us with Lady F. and her Scottish companion, our friend Cathie, who was engaged to one of Mrs Bird's sons.

They took their slow, painful walks each day to the end of the village and back. They didn't speak to us, probably because of language difficulties. In any case, we were not allowed to speak to 'strangers'.

So we didn't say hello to the Goldschmidts, and they didn't say hello to us. There was just a slight smile. I thought she was probably someone's nana.

## Albert and Thesie Goldschmidt

*According to John Oliver of the High Wych History project, these refugees were the Goldschmidts, from Bavaria, and had much of their property destroyed in the "Kristallnacht". Being German, they had to report regularly to his father, the High Wych policeman, and became friends with his mother, though Lady Foote, their host, did not think the Goldschmidts should be associating with people of a lower status. Albert passed away in 1944 and Thesie returned to Germany in 1956.*

# LAST GIRL IN

I remember I was by myself at Mrs Bird's, in my third year at HighWych. Rosie went home quite early, she was so homesick. Pat followed some time later, in or round '41 I think. Tragically, I heard quite recently, through Jean, that she was killed in an air-raid. Poor Pat Sizeland.

If it is true, then she did not have much of a chance at life. I'd like to think she'd had a few good fun times when we were together. She had to face great contrasts. I got to spend weekends with my parents. She couldn't even see her Gran, and didn't seem to have on-the-scene parents who cared about her. She was rightfully resentful.

*Patricia E Sizeland was born in Finsbury in 1930, but there is no record of her death during the war years or later. Nor is there one of her marriage either. It is possible that if she survived, she emigrated.*

# SNOW

The beautiful September days, laden with apples, blackcurrants and blackberries grew shorter and cooler. The horse chestnut trees on the village green opposite our cottage dropped their prickly green fruit and the boys quickly found out what conkers were. You squashed the green case with your boot, then extracted the smooth, brown-and-cream fruit, shiny and oily. If hard enough, the boys would drill a hole into them and thread them on string, turning them into conker treasures. Then they could be whacked against other boys' conkers to split theirs. I don't think they were edible for cattle or horses even, but when the fruit fell from its branch, it left a small horseshoe-shaped scar where it broke, hence the name, horse chestnut.

Christmas came, and Mum and Jill were installed in the caravan. I think Dad brought Nana Eastcott, Monday's Nana, down too, as she was a recent widow, I realise now, though I don't remember being told of Uncle Mike's death at the time.

We called her that since, as I understood it then, we used to see my mother's parents on a Monday, and my father's parents on a Tuesday. So their names evolved to Monday's Nana and Tuesday's Nana, since I don't remember either Grandad Willis or Uncle Mike (also my grandad, but that is what he liked to be called) being there often during our daytime visits. I don't for a moment think now that we visited every single week, but that is what I believed as a child.

In January, the snow came one night and stayed, it seemed, for weeks, floating down day after day, changing our village to white, black and grey. We London children didn't know this was unusual even for the country. London snow fell, lay briefly white in places, then turned to grey slush. Ridges made by cart-wheels, car tyres and footprints froze hard then were dusted by a thin, hopeful layer of snow which froze again, until the whole slushy mess ran down gutters and drains and was gone till the next snowfall. That was London.

The snow in our village – it became 'our village' to us London kids even after only three months – was a thick, marvellous presence that came overnight. The old apple tree branches outside our cottage window, thick with apples when we arrived, were now black and iced with snow. The earth in the chicken run was white, and the chickens peered from their wooden house, huddled together, softly clucking.

We three eight-year-olds from London (Pat, Pat and Rosie), who had not even been in the same class, hadn't even seen each other before arriving on Mrs Bird's doorstep, were in total agreement that morning. Dressed in seconds, we rushed down the rickety wooden stairs to get into the snow before it melted away. It did not do so for many weeks.

I can't remember what we used to have for breakfast. It was probably bread toasted on the range; though butter and sugar were rationed even then. Scrambled eggs when the hens were laying. That morning we couldn't wait to set off for school just a minute away. Thick snow lay on the playground and at break everyone poured out of the classrooms to play in it, their sopping wet gloves or mittens soon discarded. Snowballing was banned after a day or so because the teachers became fed up with coping with the results. We still made snowballs, huge ones, which we rolled round the playground.

The snow grew deeper and whiter each day. That winter of 1939-1940 was one of the coldest on record. At the village school, little girls wore pixie hoods (a knitted scarf sewn in the middle on one side to the length of your head, to form a hood with wraps), gloves, their thickest jumpers, boots and short skirts. Little boys wore jackets, jerseys, boots and short trousers.

The snow didn't go away. It snowed, melted slightly in the afternoons, froze at night and snowed again hard so that drifts and piles of snow began to build up alarmingly in places that were never cleared. Thick walls of snow appeared along the sides of lanes, covering the hedgerows. The headmaster and teachers forbad us to walk into them as the snow would be above our heads and treacherous – nine feet deep in some cases. Puddles and streams became thick ice. Telephone wires and tree branches broke under the weight of frozen snow. Icicles appeared on outside drains and taps. The long-handled water pump in our front garden, from which Mr B. or Sid, the lodger, pumped all our water, had to be covered with sacking.

The new game in the playground was slides, particularly among the boys, but girls were allowed as well. You chose an especially slippery piece of ground, slightly sloping, then

*Bobby and Jill with a snowman in front of the caravan, winter 1940*

simply took turns sliding along it till it became like glass. After a few days, there were dangerously slippery slides all over the playground. Every child in the school queued for turns at sliding. The little kids had little slides which they made or were helped to make. There was a crop of falls and bruises here too.

One morning we came to school and were horrified to find our slides had been sabotaged. Someone had sprinkled snow gravel over them all. How dare they, our slides! But we discovered at assembly that it was the headmaster and his cronies. They said they'd been 'asked' to stop the slides because they were dangerous, especially at night – well, we didn't use them at night, did we! – not to mention the wear on shoe leather.

I think we turned to making snowballs again, bigger and better this time, rolling them with huge effort, grandly around the playground. We found icicles to break off and try to keep. We shook snow from trees onto any unfortunate beneath them. We found old snow to crunch beneath our boots and fresh snow to scuff in, and as the thaw set in, we jumped in frozen puddles to try to crack the ice. If it didn't crack, it would often send up a spray of water from beneath the sheet of ice to drench anyone standing nearby.

We didn't make 'angels' in the snow. Our landladies were not as accommodating as our mothers. In any case, no one had washing machines or dryers then. Everything was dried or aired around a fire. At school, a huge stove surrounded by a metal railing heated the church hall, divided into three classrooms. We were allowed to put our damp shoes and gloves nearby. A steamy affair sometimes.

# TEA AT THE LODGE

Often we three were sent to Mrs. Bird's daughter-in-law, Margaret, for our after-school meal. I think we called it tea. She rented the lodge of one of the two great houses in the area, belonging to Lord and Lady B. To get there we had to walk through the Great Park surrounding the house. First, there were meadows with cattle grazing in them and groups of old, spreading shade trees. Then there was a beech wood and the glimpse of a lake, before the house itself, could be seen shining white through the trees. We never went or were invited there.

Margaret's husband, Mrs Bird's son, was away at the war. She had a little girl of two, Jasmine, and a baby of one, Maggie, and most nights, she provided a meal for all of us.

We used to play there, among the evergreen copses and outhouses, till just before dark. The cattle were in their stalls during the big snow, but we had to take care crossing the cattle grids in the snow because you couldn't see the gaps. The woods were spooky. Tall, dark beech trees stood close together and, though in autumn it had been fun to look for beech nuts, now their whole appearance changed: tall black trunks emerging from snow.

Usually we tried to pass through the wood quickly, but

that winter in the snow it wasn't easy; we had to carefully pick out the way through the snow.

Sometimes, when the others were away, I had to walk through it by myself. Thoughts of Red Riding Hood didn't help. I was petrified. We never did meet anyone at all in those woods.

Once when we were all playing by Margaret's door, a blonde woman with a 1920s hairstyle came through the walkway from the Manor to the Lodge. Margaret came to the door and became flustered and pink-cheeked. She addressed the stranger as 'milady'. 'Yes, milady', 'of course, milady'. So this was Lady B. We felt we had seen the queen. She didn't speak to us at all, though she had a pleasant enough smile. I wonder now what her life was really like. Perhaps she had other people to please.

When the snow finally melted it was miserable and cold. I got a cough, but it didn't warrant a day off school, as far as I remember. No lemons about.

# THE CHRISTENING

After school, walking from the playground to our various homes, the publican's daughter, Pam Smith , often walked with us. Her family owned 'The Half Moon' situated almost opposite Mrs Bird's cottage on the other side of the village green. She was a friendly, sociable child, no doubt living at the pub would have trimmed away any shyness on her part, and she got on well with villagers and newcomers alike.

We would discuss philosophical ideas about the war – Hitler's wickedness, his sidekicks Goering and Goebbels, the various planes, and anything else that came to our nine- or ten-year-old minds. One day, the question of our names came up: short names and nicknames. She was surprised mine was really Patricia.

'So we should call you Patricia, like you were christened.'

'But I haven't been christened, I don't think.'

'Then you don't have a proper name. You can't have a proper name if you haven't been christened.'

'But everyone is called something.'

'But you haven't been christened.'

This needed some thought. I discussed it with Mrs. Bird.

'You'd better ask your mum,' she said. 'You could be christened if you wanted to.'

'Really?'

So next weekend I brought the subject up with the parents.

'They say I don't have a proper name if I'm not christened.'

'We'll think about it.'

I don't think Dad had ever been christened, but I know Mum went through a Baptist ceremony with full immersion which she had hated. But they made a decision.

'You can be christened if you want. We thought perhaps you and Jill could both be done at the same time.'

'Oh well. OK.'

For my part, our christening entailed several visits with the Rev. Lamb, the then parish priest of the area. I remember we had a somewhat terse discussion over the name of the church services I had on one or two occasions attended when I was a Brownie.

'We called it "Mass",' I said.

'No, no, you can't call it Mass. It's just a service.'

'Yes, but we called it Mass.' (The church near Chatsworth Rd had been a 'High' church, I believe. Too close to Catholicism for comfort for Mr Lamb, perhaps.)

'Well, it's a service here. You'll be fine.'

So a date was arranged. Then there were god-parents to find. Dad had a customer-friend who lived nearby who owned a beautiful Alsatian dog called Beauty. I think Nana Eastcott and perhaps one of the aunties was another.

Jill and I were duly christened one Sunday, near Christmas 1941, at the beautiful little High Wych Parish Church of St James. Mrs Bird came, and gave me a prayer book, the English Book of Common Prayer. I still have it with her little message in it: 'To Pat, with best wishes from Mrs Bird. Xmas 1941.

My parents were there. I expect Nan Eastcott was there, and, of course, Pam Smith, who was, after all responsible for it all. I wonder if she still remembers it?

When Jill turned five, she came to live with Mrs Bird so she could attend school at High Wych. Bombs were still landing on London by then, so there was no possibility of Mum and Dad letting her go to Rushmore Rd. I remember the two of us going up to Margaret's. And I remember Jill going to High Wych School. But she was only five or so, and didn't settle. She says she does not remember being there, but she was. She only remembers going to Rushmore Rd School, opposite our shop in London.

I recall Jill was not happy and cried at school sometimes. She missed our Mum who was now back in London with my Dad. I don't think she stayed very long at High Wych because of this. I think she started school there with Miss Collis. I remember some of the children, including Pam Smith, came to me one playtime saying, 'Your sister is crying.'

I wasn't sure whether I should go to her classroom or not, or would they ask me to go, but in any case, I knew it was Mum she wanted, not me. I know it was very upsetting as she was so unhappy, and I think in the end, Mum and Dad came and took her home again.

*Pied Piper Child*

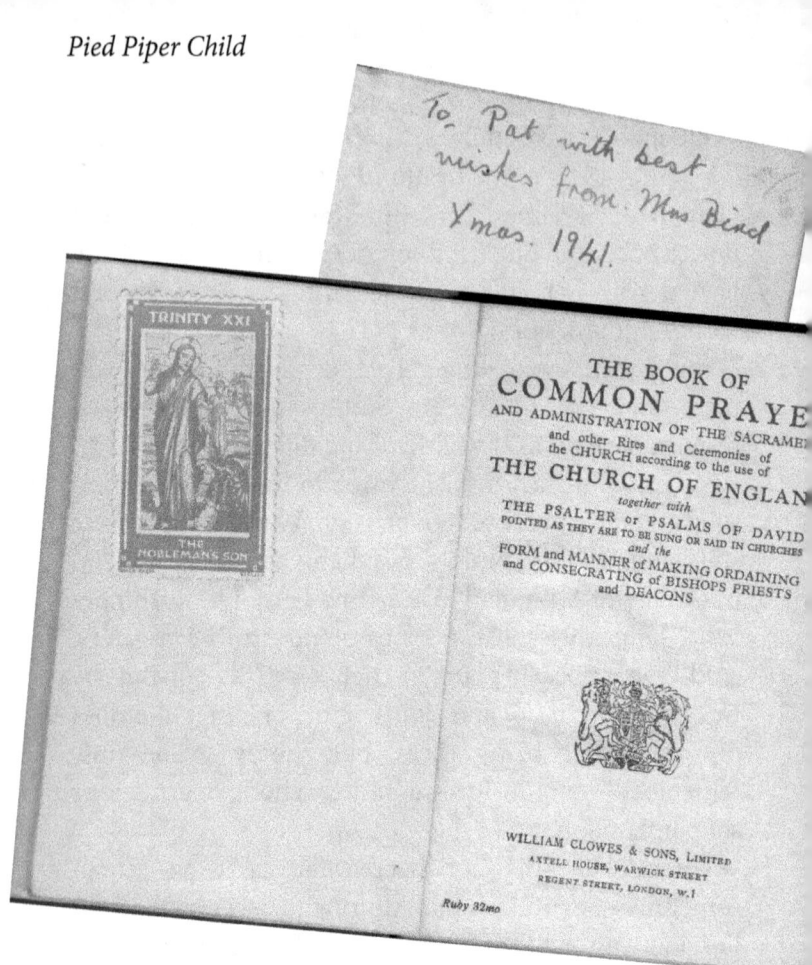

*Ria's prayer book with dedication from Mrs Bird*

# HOME: AN ENDING AND A NEW BEGINNING

After about two and a half years in High Wych, I was the only child left with Mrs Bird. I seem to remember I was happy as I could choose what to do and when. Mrs Bird was fairly easy-going, and she let me take Rex for a walk when I felt like it, which was wonderful. Dogs are such good company. One day Rex and I took our usual walk over to Redericks Farm. I knew Mum and Dad would not be there, but I felt at home there and knew the surroundings well. I manoeuvred Rex under the style, keeping him on the lead, while I climbed over the top. We walked across the fields then made our way down the muddy lane to the river meadow and walked among the buttercups there. I didn't dare let Rex off the leash as I didn't want to lose him. I was about eleven by then.

On the way back up the lane, I realised it was afternoon milking time as the herd of cows began following us. I had not left any gates open, but possibly someone had driven them towards the farm from behind and I had not seen them. Or perhaps the cows knew their own way back to the milking sheds. In any case, they spotted Rex and began to trot slowly after him at first, gathering pace, and I realised they were gaining on us. Finally Rex and I were running hell for leather up the lane, past the farm entrance, over the road and into the turnip paddock on the way back to the village. Fortunately, the cows must have turned in at the farm towards their milking stations.

Mrs Bird laughed when I told her what had happened.

'They must have thought Rex was a calf,' she said, 'and that's why they were in such a hurry.'

I seemed to spend more time with Margaret and the children. We got on well, I think. I don't remember her growling at me or anything like that, but I don't remember any conversation we had together. I had the feeling she was not happy though. I never saw her husband, nor did she, and the little girls, Jasmine and Maggie, were growing up and could talk.

During one week at school I had had to sit some sort of exam. Eleven-plus was not the rule then, but it was some sort of scholarship and I don't believe I did all that well with it. I read a lot at night, choosing my book or books from the visiting school library box, but didn't do much school work at all. Jean had gone home to her parents by then as they had moved to Hornchurch in Essex and were all together again.

I was still a stranger in the country without being aware of it. I knew the place well now, though I don't remember having much to do with other children in the village, mainly because we had always been shunted up to Margaret's at the Manor of Groves after school, and now because my two flatmates, so-to-speak, had disappeared home. Little did I know that Pat was not even on the planet by then – killed in an air-raid, it was said – and that was possibly why I was still in High Wych and so well looked after.

There was only a little post office in the village, which

sold stamps and nick-knacks, and perhaps a few sweets for the village children. So those that could, went into Sawbridgeworth for their shopping, about five miles away.

I suppose it was either delivered, or if you were lucky enough to still have or share a car, you could get your goods that way. Margaret, however, had to walk. She had the pram and once every so often she would walk with her little family into Sawbridgeworth for a larger shopping expedition. Jasmine and Maggie sometimes toddled along beside her, holding onto the pram, or sometimes shared the pram. She used to take Pat, Rosie and me with her. Now it was only me who tagged along. We were useful in staying with the children outside the shop while Margaret went inside, as she could buy her goods much more quickly by herself.

I had gone to Margaret's in the morning. Perhaps it was a summer holiday as Margaret decided we would all go into Sawbridgeworth fairly early so as to get back in time for tea. We all set out walking slowly at the children's pace at first, down the drive, over the cattle grid, through the village, past Mrs Bird's cottage. We didn't call in then, so I supposed Margaret planned to call in on the way back. We walked out of the village and up the road towards the main Harlow-Sawbridgeworth road when I heard a car behind us, an unusual event. I turned and saw to my astonishment that it was HMU 116 – Dad's maroon-coloured Morris car. I can't quite remember the sequence of events. Dad must have talked with Margaret first, I think. She came back to the pram quite ruffled and said to me,

'Did you write to your Mum and Dad?'

'No, I didn't.' I said. I was equally surprised. Then Dad

came up and said, 'We're taking you home today. Let's get in the car with Mum.'

I didn't have a chance to say goodbye to anyone. Margaret was left hurt, I believe. I didn't see Mrs Bird for a long while after that. I went to visit her while the family were staying at the caravan. I don't know what happened, or what Dad had been told or assumed. It is still a mystery as neither Mum nor Dad were generally impolite to people. I can only think they had to do everything in a hurry, perhaps to collect Jill, or perhaps it was against some silly law that they could not just take me without school permission, or something like that. I'll never know.

I knew only that within a few seconds I was in the back of the car, Mum and Dad were in front, and we were heading for home in London.

I must have left my ukulele, clothes, and a library book about a rolling pumpkin which I had not finished, at the cottage, but we didn't call in to Mrs Bird. I still feel upset about it. But they were strange times: the war was still going on, everything was scarce, and I think now that perhaps they thought Mrs Bird had somehow passed me on to Margaret. Perhaps she had – she was nearly seventy by then – though I didn't sleep at Margaret's place but at Mrs Bird's, and had a meal there at least once a day, as well as breakfast. We got on well together. And I loved Rex.

Going home was good. I belonged in London, with my own family around me and I felt things were right. But there were surprises at home. As I walked in: transformation.

At the back of the shop had been a room used as storage, filled with boxes of sweets, empty cardboard boxes, Jill's pram, and so on.

Now, through a ball-bearing door which clicked shut or open, known then as 'saloon-bar doors', a living room had materialised, decorated in warm colours: rust-coloured curtains, orange cushions, our dark oak, carved foldaway table, dining chairs, a tiled Art-Deco-style cream fireplace with a fire blazing in it, an arm-chair on each side, and further on a new kitchen, which then opened into the concrete yard and garage beyond.

And another surprise: Cliff Sisley was there, Uncle Cliff. He had laid out on the table a set of glasses, each containing a particular amount of water. He had spent some time 'tuning' the various glasses by filling them with various levels of water, so they made a musical scale and he was triumphantly able to play a tune on them with a couple of spoons.

This felt like home. I think I felt I belonged again, though I remember feeling shocked at our 'extravagant' use of electric light switches. There had been none in at High Wych – only the paraffin lamp downstairs and candles upstairs. And now, marvellously hot water was on tap.

As I look back though, I would never want to miss those years at the cottage, or the stay with Mrs Bird. The more I think about her, the more fond of her I realise I was, and the luckier I realise I was.

*Pied Piper Child*

# HOME, YES AND THEN AWAY AGAIN

## Summer 1942

### until

## Summer 1944

*Pied Piper Child*

# FIRST YEAR AT OUR LADY'S CONVENT SCHOOL

## AUGUST 1942

Long summer school holidays began in July and went on through August so there was no school when I got home. In fact, I didn't have a school not to go to. My time at Millfields (junior school) was over and I was due to go on to 'high school', (which we call 'college' here in New Zealand). I was hoping to go to a mixed school, but Mr Butler appeared again and gave advice.

'Our Lady's Convent High School for Girls at Stamford Hill is a very good school,' he said. 'Their headmistress specialises in Botany and she has an excellent reputation. They teach Latin, French, English Grammar and the various mathematics. I think it would be good for her.'

'Good for me.' So it was that I accompanied both my parents with some trepidation for an interview with the Reverend Mother Prioress, who was the headmistress of the school and the Botany expert. She was softly spoken and rather distant, probably thinking as she studied me. She asked a few questions which I don't remember and finally accepted me, despite my poor academic showing and the fact that I was not a Catholic.

> ## Our Lady's Convent
> *Our Lady's Convent High School is administered and run by an order of Servite nuns. The original order was begun in 1233, on Mt Senario near Florence, Italy, by seven men who wished to live and work in the community rather than in a monastery. The order was taken to Cuves in the north-east of France, where women joined the order and began teaching girls.*

I wore a school uniform and my new school had polished floors and nuns, Keats' 'Ode to Autumn', Latin, French, geometry and algebra – subjects I'd never heard of.

School started on August 24 that year, I think it was 1942. There was a flurry to get my school uniform together – a dismal one if ever there was one, it seemed to me then.

A black serge tunic with three large pleats falling from yoke to hem, front and back, with a blue and black girdle to tie somewhere round the middle. The tunic was worn over a white long-sleeved shirt with a thick neck tie of wide black and blue horizontal stripes. Long dark socks and black shoes, which you changed to plimsolls at school because of the polished floors. Outdoors you had to wear a round black felt hat, gloves and a dark school blazer. And no talking to boys on the way home while in uniform! The blue and white check summer frock was better but still shapeless – as close to a burka as they could manage.

On the front of the tunic you sewed a small coloured shield in the colour of your house: blue for Lourdes, mauve for Senario, green for Loretto and red for Walsingham. Lourdes, of course, was the well-known French town of miracle waters' fame, where Our Lady had appeared to Saint Bernadette. Senario referred to Mt Senario, a small mountain just north-east of Florence, Italy, where the Servite Order was founded. Loretto was the small house reputed to be where Our Lady lived. And at the time, nobody quite knew where Walsingham was.

---

## WALSINGHAM

*In Norfolk, England, Walsingham was a place of many pilgrimages in medieval times, until Henry VIII got his hands on it. Both Catherine of Aragon and Anne Boleyn, the first two of Henry VIII's wives, made pilgrimages there. Walsingham is sometimes referred to as the Nazareth of England and is now a place of pilgrimage for a wide range of Christians, including Anglicans, Catholics and Orthodox.*

I was in Walsingham – that was my house, the red one.

I see from the school website that the school uniform now is delightful –comfortable, of modern, easy-care fabrics, in an attractive shade of blue. I'm sure the girls love it. The school looks wonderful now, much larger, though the old Georgian houses seem to have gone.

I don't remember my first day at school. Perhaps my mother took me. I'm sure she did because I surely could not have coped with wearing the full uniform, getting on the right London bus and finding my way to the school entrance. I remember Dad complimenting me on my appearance, saying how smart I looked. I couldn't believe he meant it, though he probably could see a certain transformation in his daughter: from ragamuffin to schoolgirl.

I do remember being shy and taking my packed lunch out of school and down to Clapton Common to eat it as I didn't know anyone at all at the school.

From then on, getting to school involved a ten- or twenty-minute walk from home to the bus stop by Clapton Pond. There I caught a 653 double-decker trolley bus almost to the school entrance, and this took another twenty minutes or so. Most of the windows of the trolley bus were covered in a sticky green gauze with just a small rectangle of clear glass to see through, to stop the glass shattering in an air-raid. So the best seat in the bus was on the top front seat going there, and sometimes in the top back seat going home. Why the difference? I'm not sure now, but the top front seat in a London bus, in war or peace, is the best trip in England. Sometimes later on, in the summer, I cycled.

# SISTER LORETTA

Gradually I developed a liking for the surroundings and became absorbed in the teaching being given to me. The convent and school were fitted into two old high Georgian houses in fairly spacious grounds. Each had a flight of steps leading up to imposing entrances and were hidden from the road by high shrubberies.

Our classroom was on the second floor of one of the houses, large and airy, with tall windows at each side. My desk looked out onto the nuns' vegetable garden and mature deciduous trees grew to the height of our classroom, so the view changed with the changing seasons, and I felt some small connection with my former life in the country.

A world of new subjects opened up to me: new stories, books, languages, art, maths, geography, history, religious instruction, sports, gym. They held my interest. I was enthralled by most of them as they were new to me, though I struggled with some as they became more complicated later on – Caesar's endless wars in Latin, for example, and ordinary maths, though I loved geometry and algebra.

The teachers made such a difference. A teacher with

rapport can open a whole world to his or her students. I remember Sister Loretta. She had a beautifully modulated speaking voice, such as you would hear on *BBC Children's Hour* on the radio, and she would read to us during the last hour at school before we went home. She knew how to choose a book too. For her class of eleven-year-olds she chose *The Wind in the Willows* by Kenneth Grahame. (How wonderful is the internet! In looking up to check the spelling of Grahame, I found the whole story as an audio and listened to the first episode on the spot, bringing back Sister Loretta's voice, and my first weeks at Our Lady's, though it was read by Paul Honeyman.)

I have spent most of my life in Auckland, 'The City of Sails', built on a beautiful harbour, and I'm sure it is partly due to Sister Loretta's discussion sparked by Ratty's rhapsody in that first chapter:

'Believe me, my young friend, there is nothing – absolutely nothing – half so much worth doing as simply messing about in boats. Simply messing,' he went on dreamily: 'messing – about – in – boats; messing – '

'Look ahead, Rat!' cried the Mole suddenly.

Sister Loretta acted it all with her voice and actions, happily loving every minute as we all listened enthralled.

Her next choice was Dickens' *The Pickwick Papers* and the chapter describing the food they took on a picnic. An amazing description then in wartime England, as it probably was in Dickens' time in London too:

Sister Loretta also took us for English grammar, and

*An original edition of* The Wind in the Willows *by Kenneth Grahame*

English Literature, two separate subjects in those days, and so they should be always, I think, in the beginning anyway. For Grammar we had to 'parse' sentences, which involved knowing all the parts of speech and what the words did within a sentence, what a clause was, how the apostrophe worked and a myriad of small things which help to put a sentence together, and a wonderful help if you want to learn another language.

English Literature opened a wonderful world for me. Sister Loretta introduced us to poetry. It was autumn when I started there in her class, and we worked on Keats' poem 'Ode To Autumn'.

> Season of mists and mellow fruitfulness,
> Close bosom-friend of the maturing sun;
> Conspiring with him how to load and bless
> With fruit the vines that round the thatch-eves run;

I can still recite it. It is one of my favourite poems and it was so appropriate, for just outside the leaves on the tall trees were changing to yellow and orange, and I could relate that poem to High Wych and the 'thatch eaves' of Mrs Bird's cottage, and her apple tree. The cider press was a new idea.

We tackled Shakespeare too – *The Merchant of Venice* – what else?

'The quality of mercy is not strained….'

And then *Macbeth*:

'Double, double toil and trouble,

Fire, burn; and cauldron, bubble.'

followed by *Julius Caesar*: '… et tu, Brutus!'

We read through *A Midsummer Night's Dream* too, and were taken to see it at the Open Air Theatre in Regents' Park once.

The long-suffering family at home had to listen as I regaled the various quotes I could remember. I enjoyed Shakespeare and still do.

# SISTER URSULA

Then there was Sister Ursula. She was tall, with a thin, long face and big, dark eyes. She could have been Italian. She taught us geography, but for her this included astronomy and the layout of the planets. She was also very athletic. I remember one spectacular lesson where she moved some of us out of the way as she commandeered some empty desks and, hitching up her long black skirts, climbed up onto them with a globe of the earth in her hand and pointed to one of the lights in the ceiling as she demonstrated to us very graphically how the earth moved round the sun, as she clambered carefully around the light bulb, and how it turned on its own axis too. In the other hand, she had a tennis ball for the moon, though this proved difficult as she balanced precariously on our desks.

We gazed up in wonder, as much obsessed by her agility on our desk tops as in the lesson itself. We had several lessons of like nature. I seem to remember Mother Prioress walking in one day unannounced and staring up open-mouthed in amazement at her younger Sister dancing around on the desk tops, the earth upheld in one hand, and the tennis ball moon in the other. It worked very well, I must say, as I have never forgotten the lesson. Galileo would have been proud of Sister Ursula.

The school employed several lay teachers at the time. Miss Hoare (or Miss Haw) was our maths and Latin teacher. She was a wonderful teacher, extremely clear in her explanations, paying attention to every detail, which she mapped out on the blackboard and pointed at with her pointer. She was always perfectly dressed in an immaculately clean, cream frock, and spoke clearly and precisely. I did well with maths and Latin while she was our teacher. The class liked her because of her clarity and willingness to answer questions. When we progressed to a different teacher, in a later class, I began to slip as the explanations were not nearly so clear, and I floundered quite a bit.

Our French teacher was Sister Loretta again in the first year. We learned the verbs 'to be' and 'to have', the pronouns, and how to count to twenty. I loved French. In later terms, we had a Miss Skiggs as French teacher and we explored *Lettres de Mon Moulin* by Alphonse Daudet together, starting with 'La Chèvre de M. Seguin' (Mr Seguin's Goat). Miss Skiggs had an acerbic sense of humour and woe betide you if you had not completed your homework, but she had actually been to France and used to tell us a few tales of her stay there. We had no aids like CDs or DVDs to help with language in those days, not even radio, and no one could go to France because the war was still on and there was fighting there.

# SISTER FREBONIA

But my very special teacher was Sister Frebonia. That's how I remember her name, but perhaps it is not quite right.

A notice had been sent to parents to say that piano lessons were available at the school now, and I persuaded my parents to let me have music lessons. And so, Sister Frebonia and I became acquainted and liked each other very much.

She was smaller than me and very old, I thought. And she was French without a great command of English, but she had plenty of words of praise and encouragement so that I loved to go to my piano lessons. They were after school once a week and in another part of the convent.

Dad had bought an upright piano for Mum to play and it stood by the window in the drawing room, so I was lucky enough to have a room to myself to practise regularly in the evenings, generally just before the evening meal downstairs.

Sister Frebonia taught me some scales and some simple tunes, and how to read music. We enjoyed ourselves together. She loved to teach, especially as I practised enthusiastically, and I loved to learn, particularly from my own special teacher.

Sadly, one day Sister Frebonia told me she would not be teaching me anymore as she was going back to France. I don't know whether it was for the sake of her health or because she was retiring anyway, as she did seem very old, though her blue eyes always had a sparkle. I felt lost without her as I wanted to go on with my piano studies. No one replaced her at school, so Mum found a teacher nearby home, a Miss Dunkley. She was a good teacher and chose some pretty pieces, but we did not strike up a rapport. She tended to be severe and didn't smile much. I missed Sister Frebonia's Latin enthusiasm.

# OTHER TEACHERS AND AWARDS

We had a gym teacher too and a splendid gym. Mrs Selves was rather masculine, and her husband used to drape himself by the piano while he waited to take her home after school. She was good-tempered and we learned to balance on planks, climb ropes, turn upside-down on the wall bars and leap across leather horses. We played netball, though I was no great netball player.

We had a History teacher who wore blue eye shadow, rather like Mr Ball's daughter – perhaps there was only one shade back then. I often wondered how she got the job at the convent but perhaps she didn't wear make-up at the interview. We also had a rotund little science teacher, Miss Murphy, who was deaf so the class was an extremely noisy one and I didn't learn a thing, except for one spectacular afternoon when we burned all sorts of products on the Bunsen burner and had a sort of firework display. Oh yes, and there were the magnetic shavings you could make into patterns.

Religious instruction for the non-Catholics was reading stories from the Old and New Testaments. We learned passages by heart, so I added to my learning of the Ten Commandments with Mr Ball. I can now quote some beautiful passages from St Luke – especially the Christmas verses and the Sermon on the Mount. To be taught the New Testament stories by a Servite Nun was a privilege as the stories glowed with the love and the faith they had personally devoted their lives to.

There were seven types of bad marks you could get at school: silence marks (these were the most prolific), punctuality marks, behaviour marks (they meant bad behaviour), and the worst – order marks. I don't remember anyone getting one of these, but it was rumoured that if you got three order marks you were expelled. I think the sisters must have been comparatively lenient. I don't remember the names of the last three types of mark, but they were probably to do with the uniform, or not completing homework. Miss Hore would have explained them all to us very clearly in her clear voice, writing them on her blackboard and pointing them out with her pointer.

One incredible Monday morning at school, however, I received the gold and white 'Application Bar' to pin on my tunic: top marks in the school that week. I felt a glow of white and gold for a whole week, at school and at home. It seemed a crowning glory for that period. I had to give it back, of course, at the end of my reign. Top marks at school was not a regular feature for me.

So my first year at Our Lady's opened for me a treasure chest of new subjects and ideas and people, as did living back in a huge concrete city after my years in a Hertfordshire country village.

# FAMILY LIFE IN LONDON

I think we were all pleased to be together again as a family and for that reason tended to plan excursions together. Or rather my father did – he was an enthusiastic, energetic man and wanted to show Jill and me as much of the world as possible. In any case, he enjoyed the outings with us, and having the leisure to take them.

There was still severe rationing as everything was either non-existent, such as bananas and pineapples, or in short supply, such as sugar and chocolate. This meant that our shop closed now about five or six in the evening and closed altogether on Sundays. Thursday afternoons was still half-day closing for everyone in Chatsworth Rd.

Suddenly, Mum and Dad had leisure time, a real novelty. Dad picked up the guitar again. He found a teacher – a very good one in fact, Bert Weedon, a well-known guitarist of his day – and started practising in earnest.

Mum now found she could not get to her piano much, as I was always there. She gave in to me, of course, as mothers do, and after some consultation, she decided she

*Pied Piper Child*

would like to try the piano accordion.

They found a light-weight Wurlitzer for her. After all, we had another floor to fill, what with Dad in the living room with his guitar, me in the second-floor drawing room at the piano: now there was room for Mum in the bedroom. I think Jill nestled by the fire in the living room with Dad and a book. We practised for about an hour each evening and sometimes, as we progressed, came together to try out playing a song we could all do. This was the start of a new era, the start of our small band, had we known it then.

We also had the radio. *ITMA* (*It's That Man Again*) on

Sunday lunchtimes, with the then-popular comedian, Tommy Handley. Handley had devised a successful programme of introducing characters who said the same phrase every week, which seemed to make people laugh. There was the charlady who used to come on and say, 'Can I do you now, Sir?', and the Colonel who used to say, if offered a brandy, 'I don't mind if I do'. In fact, several characters said that. It became a top-up of good humour in the shop – customers would come in and say, if asked if they wanted anything else, like cigarettes or fudge, 'I don't mind if I do'. And everyone would laugh, or pretend to, which had the same effect of lifting your spirits after an air-raid. People needed to laugh, and I think there was a great understanding of this among Londoners then.

The royal family were in the news too. Princess Elizabeth came of age and joined the ATS. She was shown changing a tyre on her jeep. The Queen Mother, then the Queen, visited bomb sites and was said to have helped look for someone's cat in the rubble. Whatever the machinations of the warmongers, the people of the nation maintained a good spirit. And that was a treasure that could be felt.

And then there was Churchill. He led the country. Despite subsequent portrayals of his character, of his misdoings in his earlier life, or later, he was the right person for the job then and the English, particularly Londoners, responded to the persona he portrayed and performed well. This was no time for snide delvings. His voice on the radio, the King's voice on the radio, created a feeling that England did have some sort of leadership, some sort of chance to survive Nazism. And it worked.

# OUTINGS

We explored various trips as a family. A favourite was to drive to Southend, and either walk or take the fabulous and famous little train to the end of the 1.34 mile-long (2.16 km) pier that extended into the Thames Estuary, and walk back again. It was a breath of sea air, or salty muddy air, depending on the tide of the day. As far as I remember, there was a dance-hall at the end and various gaming machines, and, of course, a café and ice-cream kiosk. The life-boat launching station was there too.

Sometimes in the summer, we would take a trip to Kew Gardens to explore the beautifully laid-out gardens and trees, the Chinese Pagoda, and the hot houses there.

Another favourite place for a Sunday morning walk was nearby Epping Forest. We would drive there and walk the forest paths through the rust-coloured bracken and old trees, sometimes catching a glimpse of deer disappearing from sight in the distance. The forest was originally a royal hunting forest where Plantagenet and Tudor kings hunted and where no commoners were allowed to touch the deer: punishment for hunting the king's deer was death. Commoners were allowed, however, to take branches from the trees for firewood, so most of the old trees in this sort of forest have been pollarded through the centuries, which apparently helped their growth.

*Southend: a bustle of restaurants, cafes and life*

And then there was the Kingfisher swimming pool at or near Chingford, on the edge of Epping Forest. The pool tiles were turquoise, blue and yellow. I loved it. The swimming trip was mostly taken with Dad, as Mum did not much care for swimming and liked to have a little time to herself at home.

I loved going there and used to hope and pray, on a hot summer's day, walking home from school, that Dad would feel like a swim that evening. Sometimes, after a swim we would call round to Dad's sister, Elsie, who lived nearby with husband Len and her two boys, Victor and Trevor. The two families got on well, and I rather liked my cousin, Vic, though he was a few years older than me. We had played together as kids. His favourite toy before the war was a model of the Queen Mary, the latest ocean liner, with three funnels.

Elsie and Len had a pretty garden at the back of their house, and we would stay for a cup of tea and a sandwich, or biscuits. Barbecues had not been invented then, and we would not have had meat to put on them anyway.

But there was to be yet another huge interruption as the short London peace was shattered again.

*Ria's aunts Edie, Elsie and Lily (left to right, oldest to youngest) in their heyday back in the 1920s*

# THE MYSTERY PLANE
## 13 JUNE 1944

School life continued from 1942, through into 1944 with me at Our Lady's High and Jill at Rushmore Rd Primary. The war continued in Africa, Sicily, Italy, Holland and elsewhere and 'our boys' and our allies fought there, but the London Blitz had been over for some months now and it seemed as if the war was receding from England, physically anyway. I don't remember any air raids then in that period, but I believe there were quite a few since people talked about them. Perhaps I slept through them.

Then one day, the morning newspaper headlines exploded: 6th June 1944. 'Our Armies in N. France. 4,000 Invasion Ships Have Crossed Channel' said *The Daily Mail*. It was D-Day, and the Normandy beaches were being invaded. A multitude of young men died on those beaches or closer inland, but those that managed to stay alive and move further into France became the spearhead for the eventual liberation of France and Holland.

There was a glimmer of hope and I remember everyone paying rapt attention to news from newspapers and radio: Dad had two morning papers delivered, which he read at breakfast. Our daily lives in London and elsewhere went on as normal. Jill and I still went to school, people to work and shops opened as usual, albeit for shorter hours.

Then one night, only a few days after D-Day, the warning sirens sounded in the middle of the night with that awful up-and-down wailing. Jill and I were asleep in the top back bedroom. Dad grabbed his tin hat and ARP (Air Raid Precautions) coat and told Mum to get us kids to the shelter.

We were awake by then and suddenly the ack-ack (anti-aircraft) guns down on Hackney Marshes started firing. Mum got us both into one bed and lay over us herself, hoping we would not be in a direct hit. After a few seconds

---

## ARP WARDENS

*Ria's father, Charles Willis, was a volunteer Air Raid Precautions (ARP) warden throughout the war. Set up in 1937, the ARP changed its name to the Civil Defence Service in 1941, and was disbanded shortly before the end of the War in Europe. According to Wikipedia, 'ARP wardens ensured the blackout was observed, sounded air raid sirens, safely guided people into public air raid shelters, issued and checked gas masks, evacuated areas around unexploded bombs, rescued people where possible from bomb-damaged properties, etc. and called in other services as required.'*

of quiet, we got coats and shoes on, grabbed blankets, and Dad shepherded us downstairs and out the door on our way to the reinforced concrete air-raid shelter underneath a school, just one block away.

He said he always waited till our footsteps stopped and he knew we had reached safety before he set off on his rounds. He used to laugh about how our footsteps started off normal then got quicker and quicker as the guns started firing. There was almost more danger from shrapnel than from bombs.

I remember the shelter that night. A few bunks. A lady and her young sons were already sitting there. I remember her London accent. Cheerful, making room for us. As we waited, cuddling close, we heard the plane they were firing at and waited for the whistle of the bombs as the plane dropped its load of incendiaries.

But nothing happened. We waited silently. The guns had stopped. Then suddenly there was an explosion quite nearby it seemed. Had the gunners brought the plane down? We assumed they had. We could breathe easy for a while. Even try to sleep, all bundled up, for a couple of hours or so. Dad called in. All was quiet nearby, though there had been that explosion in the distance.

Finally, tired and hungry, we all decided to go home, and traipsed back to the shop. Mum made tea and cooked breakfast for us, though Dad went out again. He came back later and opened the shop as usual about 8.30 a.m.

I remember thinking, *I'm going to be really late for school today, but I'll have a really good excuse.* Mum, Jill and I were sitting round the old oak table. Jill and I were half asleep. Mum was very nervous.

Dad came down the passage and clicked open the door.

He was wearing his white coat, ready to make ice cream. He looked at Mum.

'Flying bombs,' he said. 'They're sending flying bombs over.'

Just silence.

Mum and Dad went into conference. Scared? Of course. How many? Not just night-time but day-time too. I was thirteen and a bit, Jill seven and a bit. I was thinking, well, maybe we'll have the day off school now.

## V-1 FLYING BOMBS

*That first V-1 flying bomb on 13 June 1944 had landed close to us in Mile End, London's east end, killing eight civilians. At their peak, more than one hundred V-1s a day were fired at south-east England, 9,521 in total, decreasing in number as the firing sites were overrun by allied troops. The British learned to intercept them: Operation Crossbow used both ack-ack guns and barrage balloons; then brave young pilots, as well as shooting them down, would intercept the bombs in their planes, aiming to 'topple' the bomb with a wingtip, so it veered off to land in the fields of England rather than built-up areas. The bombs were launched from the French and Dutch coasts, or from bombers.*

*A V-1 flying bomb falling on London*

No.

Dad came back.

'Go upstairs, pack your things, not many. You're all going to the caravan.'

'What, now? What about school? Holidays don't start till July'

'Yes. Now. I'll drive you down then come back.'

So that's what happened. We couldn't be left by ourselves so Mum had to come too. Money had still to be earned, and Dad was an ARP warden so he had to stay in London.

We probably packed clothes, bought food, then were on our way. We were so lucky. We still had our caravan, so had somewhere reasonably safe to go, though as it turned out, the doodlebugs, as they came to be known, were fairly uncontrollable and scattered themselves everywhere.

*ARP wardens searching V-1 bomb damage for survivors*

# BACK TO HIGH WYCH

## SUMMER 1944

*Pied Piper Child*

# THE ERRAND GIRL

Soon we were settled safely in our caravan. Fortunately, it was early summer so we were warm. We had a small in-built stove to cook on, and on which our mother produced wonders. I was detailed to fetch water from the farm in the large glass bottles we kept there. I think they were about three litres each, and quite heavy, but it was not a long trip to fill them, over a stile, through the plum orchard and into the farmyard, where there was an outside tap in a barn. The old farm dog used to bark at me when I passed him, as he was still on guard.

I felt quite happy at being back in the country again. No school and apparently no homework. No one had time or energy to think about such things. Mum was worried about Dad, and we were all curious, though in a disbelieving sort of way, about how far the bombs could travel. We would look up and closely inspect any planes that happened over us, which were quite a few as there were aerodromes nearby.

After a few days, Dad brought down my bike. In order for us to be independent, I was to be the local errand girl. I think they fixed a small basket onto the front of my upright bike, so I felt rather like the district nurse doing her rounds.

I had to cycle into Harlow to get fresh vegetables or whatever we needed. I think Dad brought down food when he could, and probably Mrs Hipwell helped us with milk and eggs. She was very good. I was thirteen and obstreperous at times and I didn't like cycling into Harlow. Yes, truly selfish. Never mind any war effort.

'But Mum, it's dangerous, and the army lorries drive really close to me and nearly knock me off my cycle.'

Well, yes they did actually, once or twice, but I exaggerated. In fact, I got to quite like doing the shopping, bringing back potatoes, lettuce and tomatoes, or whatever was needed.

'You'll be all right,' said Mum. She'd put on her 'just do it' face, and off I went without further argument. I did realise that we had to have food, me most of all.

In those days, Harlow was little more than a village, or a small town, built round the River Stort with its lock, and a basic shopping centre. No one had even a glimmering of 'Harlow New Town', which was built after the war.

Summer is the most beautiful time in the English countryside. We lived in our caravan from 14 June till the beginning of September 1944 and as I remember, it was the most wonderful summer. It's how I like to think of England now, and if I go back, it would be so disappointing to find it is no longer there.

Hedgerows still threaded their way in and around the small fields and meadows. They were full of treasures. In March were 'pussy willows' and in April yellow catkins appeared like pollen-covered lambs' tails, in the hedgerows and on hazel trees. You could suddenly come across a bush of dog-roses, single-petalled and delicate, with just a faint scent if you could get beyond their thorns to smell them.

Elderberry bushes flowered in flat creamy white heads of summery-smelling flowers, which you could smell before you actually saw them. In the meadows, besides buttercups and daisies and clover, cowslips flowered, then those ox-eyed daisies which I later discovered made my eyes water.

Next to our caravan was a hazel copse. The yellow catkins were finishing when we arrived that year, but tiny red-stamened flower buds which became nuts were just starting to appear. (Hazel has both male and female on its branches.) Hazel was grown not only for its beautiful nuts, but its branches were good for thatching spars, hurdles and furniture because the new spring branches could bend easily. Hazel has a reputation as a magical tree and I can well believe it. Its branches are used by water diviners, and a hazel rod is supposed to protect against evil spirits.

And in case you are wondering, we used the depths of the hazel copse in an emergency, learning to dig a hole then cover it again as necessary. Primitive, yes, but vitally necessary, and I like to think now that we fertilised the earth, as all our food was organic in those days. And we had the farmer's permission. He was a very practical man.

We also had a radio, so Mum had her *Henry Hall*, and Dad could listen too.

We settled into our country lives reasonably well, as we were used to caravan life. We could cope with earwig invasions, rainy days – though I can't remember many – and stepping accidentally into cow pats. We walked, played paper games and probably went to bed really early, though it was long summer nights by then.

# FRESH CARAVAN, FRESH COMPANY

Then, suddenly we had company. Les and Inez Newton and their daughter Pat, with whom we had spent summer holidays at the Shakespeare Hotel in Clacton, asked Mr Hipwell if they too could put a caravan on his farm. Mr Hipwell agreed: Les was a great talker, the leading salesman of his day, having turned Mars Bars into a best-seller.

So one weekend, a large caravan arrived. It was similar to ours as I think we had updated our caravan by then. Towed down the lane by a tractor, it was installed in a field opposite ours. They too were fleeing from the flying bombs. So suddenly I had a companion of more or less my own age, who was also happy to be off school for a long summer. We got on pretty well, though both families had come from very different backgrounds.

My father used to say Inez must have been very beautiful in her day. She was striking now, with short, honey-coloured hair, large brown eyes and an ample figure. Uncle Les I adored, though was rather in awe of him. He is a person I would love to meet now. He would talk to me on equal terms, with such a good humour that everything he said was interesting or made you smile. One of his phrases was, 'I've got the nucleus of an idea.'

Inez would pretend to groan, and we would all sit back expectantly to hear it. Inez was good at devising things for us to do. I remember her coming to visit us in our van, and getting Pat and me to sit down and play battleships. We would have to draw our own diagrams on our own piece of paper, and then play battleships as today's kids play it now on iPads and computers. It kept us quiet and busy for at least half an hour while our mothers talked. I wonder what Mum and Inez talked about. They were so different, and now they were shunted into the countryside, into a caravan on a (probably) wet day. Inez was a socialite, and used to being a guest and hostess in various situations.

*The Plume of Feathers in former times*

Mum was used to being a hostess in a very different way: cups of tea for the neighbouring shopkeepers, talking to customers in the shop, or the shop girls. But they seemed to get on. I don't think they would have continued to see each other on holidays after the war and so on if they did not get on. The two couples were good friends.

Sometimes when both men were down for the weekend, we would all walk down to a local pub. This was The Plume of Feathers at Gilston, a small hamlet just down the road, a mile or so from High Wych. (High Wych, Gilston and Redericks Farm were at the three points of a triangle, so to speak.) We would all walk the mile or so to the pub, then Pat, Jill and I would have to sit in the porch outside the pub being fed potato crisps and lemonade, while the adults would have a drink inside. Sometimes we would be allowed into the 'inglenook' inside, if we were very quiet and good. It's a great pub. Jill and I visited it a few years ago and I loved it.

It is haunted. It has dropped below the road about two feet I think, or rather the road has been built up outside it. Opposite is the Gilston Church of St Mary. Gilston has a colourful history and is well worth reading about.

I remember walking home one evening and the road was covered with tiny frogs. A seasonal thing, it seemed, and we had to be careful not to walk on them.

Uncle Les was really good at impersonating Charlie Chaplin. He could walk the walk and did so after a drink at The Plume of Feathers, walking back to the farm, avoiding the baby frogs on the road.

*Outside the Shakespeare Hotel in Clacton-on-Sea, before the war (1938): back, Charles Willis; middle, Inez Newton and Bobby Willis; front, Ria, Gerald Newton and Pat Newton*

*Charles and Ria by the sundial in front of the Shakespeare Hotel at Clacton-on-Sea before the war (1938), Charles explaining how a sundial works*

# KITH AND KISSING COUSINS

We sometimes had visitors at the weekend. They could take the train to Harlow and, if Dad had the car, he would meet them at Harlow Station and bring them down to the caravan. My cousin Vic came down once, with his new girlfriend called Pat. They went off for a walk in the countryside, little knowing that Pat Newton had suggested we follow them and spy on them. (No TV in those day, you see). I was a bit doubtful about following because Vic was family after all, but we did – though I think they were pretty canny and lost us quite soon.

Vic broke with that girl before long and started going out with a local girl called Jean, whom he knew from school. (A few years later, at a Masonic dinner I was at with Mum and Dad, he met Ann Stewart, seventeen: looking beautiful in a knock-down white, shoulderless dress she had made herself. She confidently got up and made a speech. I was impressed, so was Vic. He married her within a year, I think, and they had a long, presumably happy, marriage.)

Nana Eastcott, Ada Eastcott, visited several times, but generally came down with Dad. He would have collected her on his way. She really enjoyed the visits and got on well with

Dad, whom she called Charlie, and we were always pleased to see her. She seemed to be our only available grandparent. Uncle Mike had died, and I never saw Grandad and Nana Willis during those years.

Dad's youngest sister, Lily, came down once with her new husband, Bill, who had enlisted in the RAF and was on his last leave before embarking overseas. They had no children. We never saw him again. We learned later that he was on the hospital ship which was sunk just off Singapore, in the Java Sea, by the Japanese. He was at first reported missing and Auntie Lily waited years to know what had happened. Finally she met Eric and they were married once Bill's death was eventually confirmed.

Those weeks living in the caravan through to the end of June, and all of July, the whole, lovely summer, were memorable. Looking back, we were living through the last of an era. It was an almost dreamlike existence. No school. No routine. Can't think how, if ever, we kept clean – probably swimming in the river at weekends, where someone had made a small public swimming pool in a back bend of the river. Warm enough for even Mum to venture in and Jill to be shown how to cling to the handrail built round the children's enclosure. Then we would walk back along the river bank, cross the riverside meadow and up through the hedge into the square field to the caravan.

Dad had become good at cooking too by then. He could turn on a hearty breakfast: eggs, bacon perhaps, depending on Soapy Joe, and by the end of the summer, mushrooms, gathered that morning from near the van.

He could make 'parkin', a sort of gingerbread made with oats, which you could eat as a cake or as a dessert. I think it did not require much sugar. He pickled walnuts when they were plentiful, and I think he once made apple chutney. Jill and I, especially me, required a lot of feeding by then.

Sometimes we went across the narrow lane, rutted by the daily milking herd, to the Newtons' van in the next field. They had a very different view to ours. The van was parked at the top corner of the field, by the gate, overlooking a large wheatfield, sloping down to the river meadow. We had watched the wheat that year grow from short green shoots to taller green shoots. Then the seed head opened and changed colour from pale green to almost white, before slowly turning to a dry white-gold on a slender stem. You could pluck the head from a stalk and eat a few of the hard seeds, enclosing white flour, not because they were tasty, but because we could. It was a classic wheatfield: mauve scabious flowers appearing amongst the green, followed, as the wheat ripened, by beautiful blue cornflowers, white, yellow-centred ox-eyed daisies, purple vetch, yellow mustard plants and finally the traditional scarlet corn poppies. All of these flowers appeared, through summer, scattered around the edges of the field, or amongst the wheat crop, enjoyed by birds, bees, field-mice and plenty of unseen others no doubt. But none of it lasted. Ripe wheat has to be cut urgently before any weather destroys it.

One morning early, there was a loud rumbling and roaring down the lane near our van and when Jill and I rushed to look, we saw the threshing machine moving into Les and Inez's field. Harvest time. The machine of its day, perhaps it was a combined harvester, I'm not sure. It went slowly along the edges of the beautiful field, slashing and binding the corn, and throwing the bound bundles onto the ground behind it. Following the machine, men were picking up the bundles and stacking them in small, pyramid-shaped stooks to drain and

*A threshing machine in Nonington, Dover, during WWII*

dry before being collected. What a traditional, beautiful, Van Gogh sight. (I hate the black or pale-green plastic wrapped bundles that have taken their place, albeit they are far more practical and weather-proof.)

Then a day or so later, along the lane came the magnificent Clydesdales – two of them drawing a heavy, four-wheeled, flat-topped cart. Driving the horse was Peter Hipwell, the farmer's teenage son. At thirteen, my romantic teenage heart did a flip as I gazed tongue-tied at this marvellous sight. Men loaded the cart with the stooks and took them off to where, I'm not sure. I just remember this fabulous sight of the horses, the stooks and the young man. I think if I'd been less shy I could have had a ride on the cart, but perhaps not. The harvest had to be brought in before the weather changed.

# FINAL FAREWELLS

I remember the last time we went to the caravan at Redericks Farm.

I sometimes used to walk over the fields again to visit Mrs. Bird. I had not been for some months, and I think I knew we were moving away by then.

'Is Mr Bird up at the allotment?' I asked her.

'Mr Bird died a few months ago,' She replied.

I was stunned. I didn't know what to say, just felt guilty because I had not kept in touch. I asked after Margaret.

'We don't see much of each other now,' Mrs Bird replied. 'She's got another baby.'

'Really? I might go on and visit her while I'm here.'

I said goodbye to Mrs Bird and set off for the Manor of Groves.

Margaret was sad.

'She's not speaking to me much these days. I have a new partner and a child with him.'

I was happy for Margaret, but sad for Mrs Bird. She came from a Victorian generation, when things were

*Pied Piper Child*

very different. I wished I had had time to call in again on my way back to the caravan, but I didn't. I wish now I had.

I hope Jasmine and Maggie still called in to see her on their way home from school.

Mrs Bird was a great lady. I miss her even now. How good it would be to be able to catch up with those who have passed on, just for a chat and a cup of tea.

*High Wych Green in the early 1900s*

# WELWYN GARDEN CITY

The war took a more devastating turn in September 1944. Just as the British thought they had mastered the art of stopping the doodle-bugs from landing on cities, a deadlier missile arrived in the form of the V-2 rockets. With no warning whatsoever, these just fell and exploded, fired from somewhere in Europe. Long-range and deadly, they could not be stopped like the doodlebugs.

The British Government, including Churchill, told the public it was probably a gas leak explosion, but the public were not fooled. Typical Cockney humour discussed the 'deadly flying gas pipes'. Everyone knew it was a German weapon.

The world's first guided ballistic missile was made by concentration camp labourers in Germany under forced labour regimes where thousands were killed. Over 3,000 were launched against London and other targets, but not until November 1944 were the public told they were under rocket attack.

Meanwhile our safe caravan, only twenty-five or so miles from London was not really a safe haven any more. Also, life had to go on. School loomed. Our Lady's had, all through

the war, had a part of its school in Welwyn Garden City, presumably evacuated there at the beginning of the London Blitz. That seemed to be the destiny and destination for Jill and me.

'Well, why can't we just stay here? We can study here at home. I don't want to go to Welwyn. And there's no piano there. And Jill won't like it.'

That I knew to be true. Jill liked to be within the family, near Mum.

But there was no arguing. Bombs were dropping, and presumably the law, ass like it usually is, said we had to be at school. And Mum wanted to be with Dad who needed help in the shop.

So, it was Welwyn Garden City for us, sometime in September or October 1944. A billet had been found for us with a Mrs Turner. I can't remember how we got down there. Perhaps Dad drove us, perhaps we went by train. Perhaps I was there for a few weeks before Jill. It's all fairly vague now.

We were greeted by Mrs Turner, a round, buxom woman, kindly disposed. She kept a very clean house, as I discovered when I came home on Friday afternoons to find the floor covered in newspapers so as to keep it clean for the weekend. Mr Turner was fairly talkative. He had spent some years in the Far East once, and had carvings in the living room to prove it. He took a cold bath every morning, for his health's sake, he said.

They looked after me and fed me well, and made sure my clothes were clean, and I had my own room, though to this day I can't remember what it was like. I didn't know what was missing at the time, but I think now it was a sort of intelligence, a sense of humour perhaps. Mrs Bird had it. I could have a laugh with her. Mrs Turner did not.

Welwyn Garden City was and is one of Britain's newest cities, built after World War One. It was designed as a series of circles, so that houses were built in a circle with a green centre for community use. It was a good, well thought-out design, except that there were too many of them. It made the city look the same all over. There was a huge factory near the railway station built to manufacture shredded wheat, so of course, its product was called Welgar Shredded Wheat.

One of the local schools had given over a couple of its classrooms to Our Lady's, when children had arrived at the beginning of the war during the first evacuations with Sister Alban, who was still in charge. I don't know how I got there the first day. Perhaps Mrs Turner took me, perhaps someone called for me. I think it was just me and that Jill had not yet arrived.

I met Sister Alban. I had been my own boss and my own self for months and here was Sister Alban watching me all the time. Or so it seemed. I think she was just a very concerned teacher, with only a few charges now, who herself did not want to be where she was, so I think she was overly strict in an attempt to create some order in our lives.

In London and south-east England, the Germans started to send over rockets in place of the predictable doodle-bugs. A rocket sent from France or Holland could land at anytime, anywhere, during day or night, and they had more explosive power than the doodle-bugs. The first rocket landed on September 8 1944 and continued through November, the final one landing in March 1945. Some killed only two or three, though leaving huge craters and building damage. Another hit a Woolworth's store, killing hundreds.

Mum came down to see me one weekend and brought my bike on the train. I think we had a walk in the town and an ice-cream perhaps till she had to catch the train back. She did bring me good news: we were all going to spend Christmas at Clacton at the old Shakespeare Hotel, with our friends, Les and Inez, and some others. There was going to be a dance, and she would make me a dress. I was thrilled. It was something to look forward to.

Jill came down at some time, either for a short while, or after Mum's visit. I know I used to cycle to school after that, and she had to walk. I said she was too young to get the bus, or something like that, so she had to walk. Why all the adults concerned took my word for it, I don't know. Mrs Turner or Sister Alban could easily have told her to get the bus. Probably I was a really bolshie thirteen-year-old, always on the edge of melt-down, likely to decide to just walk home to London at the slightest word, so they left well alone and Jill suffered.

One day I do remember. There was a girl my age billeted in the same circle of houses. We got talking. Her name was Mitzi. I think now she was probably from Austria or somewhere similar. She had a bike and we decided to go for a ride one Saturday afternoon. It was a lovely day, and we cycled out of Welwyn and on the road to Hertford. I had been there once with Mrs Bird years ago.

Whenever I see that well-known picture of two girls in long dresses on upright bikes, wearing summer hats or something, I think of the two of us on that day, happy to be free of our lodgings, of school, and on the road to nowhere. We got on well. Shortly after that, she left, or I left, and we lost touch. We didn't get to Hertford as it was rather far, so we had to turn back, but it was a good day.

There was a boy next door. I never saw him, but they told me his name was Alan. The Turners used to tease me about him and threaten to introduce me. So uncool (as my granddaughter would say). If they'd left things alone, we might have knocked into each other, but everything was so observable by the Turners.

Winter came and we played netball in the rain on a slippery court – with Sister Alban watching. I played hockey for the first time and loathed it. I didn't enjoy team sport. In fact, I didn't enjoy sport at all till I got to play tennis in my later teens.

The rocket bombardment of London and south-east England continued. Jill and I lived through the grey days, hoping some things would improve, perhaps the war would end, you never knew. We should have been happy not to be in London, but we weren't. We were temporary refugees, comfortable but dissatisfied. We were just ploughing along, ungratefully.

# CLACTON AND THE SHAKESPEARE AGAIN

Mum's coming had given us something to look forward to. Christmas at Clacton – Clacton-on-Sea that is, the place where we used to go pre-war. The Newtons were coming, Nana Eastcott was coming, and some other friends. There would be dances, and Mum had promised to make me a frock – a dance frock. (Yes, you New Zealand grandkids, that means a long dress – different words for different worlds. Get used to it!)

Somehow we got to the end of that term and were taken home. I think the rocket attacks had subsided somewhat as their bases were captured by the allies. I don't remember how we got home, or arriving back at Chatsworth Road, but we were home and then on our way to Clacton.

I certainly remember that 1944 Christmas. The old Shakespeare Hotel had not changed, even the sundial was still in the front garden. I shared a room with Pat; I think Jill was with Mum and Dad. Dances were held for several evenings. A Miss St John and her trio played for them, with Miss St John herself on the upright piano. I think she had drums and a sax making up the trio, playing on a small raised dais.

Mum had put together an outfit for me by taking a full white net skirt, probably from a pre-war dress of hers, decorated with red spots dotted round the edge, and had knitted a silky white, boat-necked top, with embroidered red medallions round the neckline. I wore make-up for the first time – probably just lipstick and powder, and white sandals. I hardly knew myself. As I came carefully down the stairs, Dad was watching from the floor, and said, 'Pat, you look beautiful.' This time he said the right thing.

The rellies made a fuss of me. Uncle Bert was there, and Uncle Dob too. Clacton is not so far from London, after all. Dad danced with me, as did the uncles. I even danced with my Nana and while I did, Uncle Bert came up to us and told her he was sorry. I'll never know for what, but Nana was very pleased and happy about it.

We danced all the old-fashioned comedy dances of the day: The Lambeth Walk, the Hokey-Cokey, Hands, Knees, etc. As well as more romantic waltzes and quicksteps and foxtrots. I didn't know the latter dances, but then neither did anyone else, so we managed. I have a natural sense of rhythm anyway.

It was unusual fun – family, friends and children together, after years of having to be separate. Music to dance to, food to eat, drinks to drink. I was not going to go back to Welwyn.

We didn't. We stayed home. Jill went back to Rushmore Rd school, and I went back to the Convent at Stamford Hill. Enormous relief! Family all together again. And the allies seemed to be winning the war. Could it be true?

There were terrible, haunting pictures in the morning newspapers of Belsen being freed. Skeleton-like men

*The Willis Swing Band (left to right): Cliff Sisley on double bass, Jill Willis on vocals, Bobby Willis on accordion, Billy Cutting on the drums, Charles Willis on guitar and Ria on piano and vocals*

trying to greet their liberators. Awful pictures. We heard Hitler had committed suicide. Winston Churchill accepted the defeat of Germany on 8 May 1945. VE Day – Victory in Europe – was announced.

I remember standing by myself in our drawing-room, with a sense of relief, true, but thinking, *But everything is the same.* There were no fireworks, or people dancing or shouting, not in Chatsworth Rd anyway. But soon there were street parties, as each street realised things would be different and localities gradually came back to life.

One Sunday, the church bells began ringing again.

People were cheerful. Our little band was booked for a street party in Rushmore Rd. More parties began to happen.

I believe it was very different in central London, along The Mall, in Piccadilly Circus and Trafalgar Square. That's where the celebrations happened. VE military parades took place, with returning soldiers marching through the City and so on.

By then I was just fourteen and Jill just eight, beginning to be more settled in at home.

Japan was far away. War was still going on. Japan had not surrendered. Then in the morning newspapers one day: Hiroshima.

I don't think anyone celebrated. Our world had truly changed, that such a horror could exist. On the other hand, there was world peace. Or so they said. A VJ Day was announced – victory over Japan. And a second round of celebrations took place in the city, but in a much more sombre mood.

# The End

*The Willis Swing Quartet business card*

# Appendix
# Ria's Favourite Poems

### BERRIES
*Walter De La Mare*

There was an old woman
Went blackberry picking
Along the hedges
From Weep to Wicking.
Half a pottle –
No more she had got,
When out steps a Fairy
From her green grot;
And says, 'Well, Jill,
Would 'ee pick 'ee mo?'
And Jill, she curtseys,
And looks just so.
'Be off,' says the Fairy,
'As quick as you can,
Over the meadows
To the little green lane,
That dips to the hayfields
Of Farmer Grimes:

Ria Booth

I've berried those hedges
A score of times;
Bushel on bushel
I'll promise 'ee, Jill,
This side of supper
If 'ee pick with a will.'
She glints very bright,
And speaks her fair;
Then lo, and behold!
She has faded in air.

Be sure old Goodie
She trots betimes
Over the meadows
To Farmer Grimes.
And never was queen
With jewellry rich
As those same hedges
From twig to ditch;
Like Dutchmen's coffers,
Fruit, thorn, and flower –
They shone like William
And Mary's bower.
And be sure Old Goodie
Went back to Weep,
So tired with her basket
She scarce could creep.
When she comes in the dusk
To her cottage door,
There's Towser wagging
As never before,
To see his Missus

So glad to be
Come from her fruit-picking
Back to he.
As soon as next morning
Dawn was grey,
The pot on the hob
Was simmering away;
And all in a stew
And a hugger-mugger
Towser and Jill
A-boiling of sugar,
And the dark clear fruit
That from Faërie came,
For syrup and jelly
And blackberry jam.

Twelve jolly gallipots
Jill put by;
And one little teeny one,
One inch high;
And that she's hidden
A good thumb deep,
Half way over
From Wicking to Weep.

## THE ADVENTURERS
*Henry Newbolt*

Over the downs in sunlight clear
Forth we went in the spring of the year:
Plunder of April's gold we sought,
Little of April's anger thought.

Caught in a copse without defence
Low we crouched to the rain-squall dense:
Sure, if misery man can vex,
There it beat on our bended necks.

Yet when again we wander on
Suddenly all that gloom is gone:
Under and over through the wood,
Life is astir, and life is good.

Violets purple, violets white,
Delicate windflowers dancing light,
Primrose, mercury, moscatel,
Shimmer in diamonds round the dell.

Squirrel is climbing swift and lithe,
Chiff-chaff whetting his airy scythe,
Woodpecker whirrs his rattling rap,
Ringdove flies with a sudden clap.

Rook is summoning rook to build,
Dunnock his beak with moss has filled,
Robin is bowing in coat-tails brown,
Tomtit chattering upside down.

Well is it seen that every one
Laughs at the rain and loves the sun;
We too laughed with the wildwood crew,
Laughed till the sky once more was blue.

Homeward over the downs we went

Soaked to the heart with sweet content;
April's anger is swift to fall,
April's wonder is worth it all.

## LONDON SNOW
*Robert Bridges*

When men were all asleep the snow came flying,
In large white flakes falling on the city brown,
Stealthily and perpetually settling and loosely lying,
Hushing the latest traffic of the drowsy town;
Deadening, muffling, stifling its murmurs failing;
Lazily and incessantly floating down and down:
Silently sifting and veiling road, roof and railing;
Hiding difference, making unevenness even,
Into angles and crevices softly drifting and sailing.
All night it fell, and when full inches seven
It lay in the depth of its uncompacted lightness,
The clouds blew off from a high and frosty heaven;
And all woke earlier for the unaccustomed brightness
Of the winter dawning, the strange unheavenly glare:
The eye marvelled—marvelled at the dazzling whiteness;
The ear hearkened to the stillness of the solemn air;
No sound of wheel rumbling nor of foot falling,
And the busy morning cries came thin and spare.
Then boys I heard, as they went to school, calling,
They gathered up the crystal manna to freeze
Their tongues with tasting, their hands with snowballing;
Or rioted in a drift, plunging up to the knees;
Or peering up from under the white-mossed wonder,
'O look at the trees!' they cried, 'O look at the trees!'
With lessened load a few carts creak and blunder,

Following along the white deserted way,
A country company long dispersed asunder:
When now already the sun, in pale display
Standing by Paul's high dome, spread forth below
His sparkling beams, and awoke the stir of the day.
For now doors open, and war is waged with the snow;
And trains of sombre men, past tale of number,
Tread long brown paths, as toward their toil they go:
But even for them awhile no cares encumber
Their minds diverted; the daily word is unspoken,
The daily thoughts of labour and sorrow slumber
At the sight of the beauty that greets them, for the charm they have broken.

## NICHOLAS NYE
*Walter de la Mare*

Thistle and darnell and dock grew there,
And a bush, in the corner, of may,
On the orchard wall I used to sprawl
In the blazing heat of the day;

Half asleep and half awake,
While the birds went twittering by,
And nobody there my lone to share
But Nicholas Nye.

Nicholas Nye was lean and gray,
Lame of leg and old,
More than a score of donkey's years
He had been since he was foaled;
He munched the thistles, purple and spiked,
Would sometimes stoop and sigh,

*Pied Piper Child*

And turn his head, as if he'd said,
'Poor Nicholas Nye! '

Alone with his shadow he'd drowse in the meadow,
Lazily swinging his tail,
At break of day he used to bray,-
Not much too hearty and hale;
But a wonderful gumption was under his skin,
And a clean calm light in his eye,
And once in a while; he'd smile:-
Would Nicholas Nye.

Seem to be smiling at me, he would,
From his bush in the corner, of may,-
Bony and ownerless, widowed and worn,
Knobble-kneed, lonely and gray;
And over the grass would seem to pass
'Neath the deep dark blue of the sky,
Something much better than words between me
And Nicholas Nye.

But dusk would come in the apple boughs,
The green of the glow-worm shine,
The birds in nest would crouch to rest,
And home I'd trudge to mine;
And there, in the moonlight, dark with dew,
Asking not wherefore nor why,
Would brood like a ghost, and as still as a post,
Old Nicholas Nye.

# REFERENCES & ACKNOWLEDGEMENTS

Much of the fact-checking and photographs appearing in *Pied Piper Child* were sourced from a fabulous local resource: the High Wych History Project, run by Theo van de Bilt. I am indebted to this veritable mine of information on High Wych for the photographs of Mrs Bird (pp. 24 & 29) and the historical photos of High Wych (pp. 60 & 126) as well as Rose Pocock's recollections (p. 30). You can read more about this village here:

*http://vandebilt.co.uk/history/*

I would also like to acknowledge the British Library as the source for most of the wartime pamphlets and posters used to illustrate this book, many of which can be found here: *http://www.bl.uk/learning/timeline/item107597.html*

If any image or information used here has not been duly acknowledged, please contact the publisher, Poble Sec Books, so that we may rectify it. This book is published for non-commercial purposes. Where a price may appear on a commercial website, the intent is solely to recoup printing costs.

Lastly, Ria sets down these memories as 'how I remember them' or in Doris Lessing's words: 'Memory isn't fixed. It slips and slides about.' So where, for example, the High Wych blog records 175 evacuees and Ria recalls they were a group of about 30, I have left the discrepancy. This is, after all, a memoir not a textbook.

—*Kevin Booth, editor, Poble Sec Books*

*Pied Piper Child*

www.ingramcontent.com/pod-product-compliance
Lightning Source LLC
LaVergne TN
LVHW012108070526
838202LV00056B/5663